Sex
Love & Pain

METHODS II THE MADNESS

STEVEN A BARTHELL

AZIZA
PUBLISHING

Sex, Love & Pain: Methods To The Madness

An Aziza Publishing Book/ published by arrangement with the author

PRINTING HISTORY
Aziza Publishing Paperback Edition/ February 2014

Copyright © 2014 Steven A Barthell

Cover and Interior Design by ReBelle Design Studio

For more information write to: Aziza Publishing LLC
www.AzizaPublishing.com

ISBN: 9780988176799

The Aziza Publishing is a registered trademark.

PRINTED IN THE UNITED STATES OF AMERICA

Table of Contents

In The Midst of It All

Totally different place in life right now.....God is so good....I have learned to look forward and not in the past.....I have a lovely wife to be who prays with me, believes in me and supports me 110%....a great little girl who I claim as mines who gives me energy and life... and a son on the way (as of writing this piece) who made me just love life even more.

What we don't do as people is fully move on with our lives....we love to dwell and stay mad, sad, depressed, "over it" or just stagnant. We don't move forward for whatever reason even though the universe and the rest of the world is doing so. This is why I decided to never write about the past again when it comes to relationships or anything that isn't helping my growth as a man, writer and entrepreneur. This book is dedicated to the people who are growing through the struggle with love, growth and pain.

I have a woman who I L-O-V-E LOVE! I mean in every way we connect better than Voltron machines and our souls intertwine during prayer and meditation. A true blessing....In all honesty it just happen! Nothing was planned in any way shape or form. I had no intentions of being in another relationship for a while after my last one. But God said "my son this who I want you with" and now we have a beautiful growing baby boy on the way and a lovely daughter. I don't do the "step" crap or force anything I am just doing what I am suppose to do as a man, father and son of Christ...I am not perfect! Far from it but this "place" I am in is spectacular! Breath taking and just amazing in every way possible.

I am on the verge of conquering one of my biggest fears of tomorrow. I have been through storms, typhoons and more to get here....nobody can ruin this for me! Not a damn soul... Truth is I have censored myself A LOT! Truth is I am glad I am in a better position than I have been in years thanks to patience and faith.... Truth is I still get angry over a few things that were said about me and too me...and Truth is I am blessed to move on.

I dedicate this book to my grandparents Jetta Gilbert, Hester Mae White, Lena Taylor, Harry Gene Barthell, Charles Taylor & Prezzy White. Also to my late cousin/brother Anthony White Jr. with $2 going towards a scholarship in his name for every book sold.

To my "why" Denetra, Nevaeh & Steven Jr. I love you!

My parents, sister and brothers along with multiple members of the Barthell, White, Taylor, & Thomas clans. Tons of friends & family.

THANK YOU FOR BELIEVING IN ME

*L*adies & Gentlemen of our society its been 2 years since I have released "Women R Stupid & Men R the Reason" and we are still messing up. I still love each and everyone of you but our choices, motives, & thought process has increased to levels of stupidity that can only exist in a fantasy world. We are still not setting a great example for our children, we are still not setting the bar for healthy relationships and we are still not getting why we were placed on this earth! I introduce to you the Methods of The Madness and share once again how we can come together and be the generation that we brag about via social networks and in our heads. We will talk about how Sex, Love & Pain changes our lives, how we allow the three elements to dictate how we will, act and feel. We will get into an active conversation throughout the book on how we can break the cycle.

In this book I will finally show you how to get rid of the R.A.A.T's in our lives the people with ridiculous annoying ass tendencies something I failed to do in my first book. I will give you the rules of being single and teach you how to stop providing False Advertisement to one another just to gain popularity, a mate or friends you probably do not need. During the "Methods of II the Madness" you will once again be sucked into the world of my past and also my current present with continued tales from my life and early stages of writing my first book "Women R Stupid & Men R the Reason", you all know I have nothing to hide nor do I have anything to lose. I will point out how to stop looking for things you do not need and how we need to pay attention to the buried treasure in the world by Working Hard & the Loving Harder and that we all have to Man Up or STFU!

My generation really needs to pay attention because most of the things we are experiencing as adults is just the beginning! We will travel through some of my lazy moments and how I used the term Pain Is Temporary & allowed me to change my health and attack the gym. We are on deck NOW and we are swinging and missing at every chance we get to break the cycle of the negativity we are putting ourselves through. We are scared for no damn reason; OK I take that back there probably is a reason you are scared to move on with your life, live your life and take control of your life. Pay attention to how I emphasize the word YOUR because YOU are in control of YOUR life at all times. What we have a tendency of doing is giving a person or people more power than they should really have over us. I'm going to provide great techniques of letting some go with The Art of the Breakup. We discussed most the topics in "Women R Stupid & Men R the Reason" we discussed this on www. stevenbarthell.com we continually chat back and forth via twitter @StevenABarthell. YOU KNOW ALL OF THIS ALREADY, but we refuse to take action why? Because we're scared! Lets look at the word "Fear" for a moment. In the Webster's dictionary fear is defined as An unpleasant emotion caused by the belief that someone or something is dangerous, likely to cause pain, or a threat. What the dictionary fails to admit is fear is also a state of mind, its a habit not worth picking up just like smoking cigarettes or kicking kids at the park, and fear is something that can be overcome with courage and persistence. The fear in our society and my generation is quite scary (no pun intended) because I actually fear we will not overcome it; but there is hope and there is a way to get through this. But just as I stated in my previous book YOU ARE NOT IN THIS ALONE! You are not the only one who is going through the problems you are going through; but you are the one who has to face it and overcome it.

A famous quote from the movie "Coach Carter" starring Samuel L. Jackson uses a quote from the book *Return to Love: Reflections on the Principles of "A Course in Miracles"* by Marianne Williamson, states:

"Our deepest fear is not that we are inadequate. Our deepest fear is that we are powerful beyond measure. It is our light, not

our darkness, that most frightens us. Your playing small does not serve the world. There is nothing enlightened about shrinking so that other people won't feel insecure around you. We are all meant to shine as children do. It's not just in some of us; it is in everyone. And as we let our own lights shine, we unconsciously give other people permission to do the same. As we are liberated from our own fear, our presence automatically liberates others. "

I love that poem and its a great inspiration to our lives. Some of us fear that we will be successful, some of us fear we will be happy and not worry about anything bad happening, we fear that someone may actually loves us, we fear that we will lose, we are afraid that we will not get our way, we fear living and we fear LIFE! Lets walk together in this book on how to break this fear! For one it starts with effort. Most of us want the happiness, success and love and expect not to put in the work or effort! Yes I am yelling via typing again because this pisses me off to the fullest; we are spoiled and we are lazy. One of the people I watch and read on the regular is Eric Thomas and he said it loud and clear. He states in his videos via YouTube and his book **The Secret To Success,** *"When you want to be successful as bad as you want to breathe, then you'll be? successful!"* tons of us are afraid of our own success as we can not handle the responsibilities that come with or the problems, yes the problems. I'll give you another quote from someone on an even higher level Christopher "Notorious B.I.G" Wallace made it into a famous song and line the Mo' Money the Mo' problems we face! Its true, its damn true. In the very first chapter we are going to dig deeper into fear and how we can over them. How talking will only take us so far, sometimes it is best to shut the f*** up and man up. Thank you once again for digging deeper and seeing why I am the way am I am. The madness that overcomes my logic and the words I share on a daily basis on various social networks: Twitter, Facebook & Google +. Its time to travel into my mind and discover why I am crazy to name a book "Women R Stupid & Men R the Reason" or why in the previous book I used so much profanity and was open to the word "nigga" as frequently as I was. We are going to take the voyage through my soul and I will share my secrets about myself and life. Once again some things I am not proud of and other things I have no regrets on. God doesn't make any mistakes; but we do! I give you the "Methods II The Madness"

- *Steven*

Power of the D.I.C.K
Deceptive Intuition Causing Khaos

I stated in my first book Women R Stupid & Men R the Reason that "we are all f***ing up" I also stated that its our responsibility as a generation to be accounted for all our mistakes and bad decisions. It's said that the definition of insanity is doing the same thing over and over again and expecting different results. So yes, we know that snooping around our spouse's Facebook account is a bad idea, that believing in the fairy-tale love stories we grew up reading is silly, but sometimes we find ourselves giving these relationship moves the ol' college try! The results? Not so successful. Plus, we start to feel unbalanced, and sometimes just plain ole stupid!

The point is this, there are certain relationship mistakes women make over and over again. Like sleeping with someone right away because they believe it will eventually turn into a commitment or that they can change a man because "they are different" or the myth that if she caters to his ego he will realize that she is the woman he has been searching for his entire life when in reality she is just creating a fantasized notion that will reveal itself in a few months. Well it's time to stop! Quit the terrible idea that you can change a man or that you can force him into marrying you etc. Quitters sometimes prosper, especially when lousy habits get left behind. Don't worry I will get on the men in this chapter as well.

What irks me more than ever are those women who change because they are getting good sex. The good D.I.C.K they are getting is nothing but a Deceptive Intuition Causing Khaos at times yes Khaos with a "k". We'll get more into as we go deeper into this chapter but here is a list of things most men believe women should stop doing.

1. Thinking you'll never get over him or her. YOU will! Two months and several Facebook posts later... you'll feel better when you realize "shit I am still living despite feeling I could never live again without this person".

2. Hacking into email or phones looking for suspicious messages and then yelling at him for the "k thnx bye" text he sent to his female co-worker two months ago. "k thnx" is not code for "hot steamy sex." (Is it?)

3. Thinking your partner must be interested in everything you do, think and say! When it comes down to it, some women zone out when men talk about sports & other manly things right? Having a best friend or jibberish partner as (my uncle would say) outside a relationship is a good thing! Yes he is suppose to be your best friend BUT driving him insane because he refuses to watch "Love & Hip-Hop" or listen to your favorite artist will get you nowhere.

4. Displacing! If you're mad at him because he ate your tasty restaurant leftovers out of the fridge, tell him you're mad at him because he ate your tasty restaurant leftovers out of the fridge! Don't turn it into a commitment issue. "You are so inconsiderate! You don't love me because you cant sacrifice your hunger" Please have a seat. Make that several seats.

5. Putting so much energy into the idea of a fairy-tale romance that you get disappointed with anything less. As a man I hate this shit and I know other guys do as well. This is our life! Not Snow White, not a bunch of glitter vampires, or Cinderella.

6. Waiting for someone to find you, instead of going out and finding someone yourselves. Thing is YES a husband seeks a wife but if you stay cooped in the house what is there to seek?

7. Thinking that a perfect relationship should be easy. Relationships require work and compromise; a perfect relationship means doing those things consistently.

8. Dropping your friends when you're falling in love. Friends help define who you are, and you need them when things get tough or if you need to vent about your relationship. Just be careful about what you share with your friends. We love the fact you have friends, that means when its Game 7 and you are not interested you can go with your friend or friends and leave use the hell alone.

9. Thinking that getting a boyfriend or husband will solve all your problems. No one can fix your lives for you but you!

10. Using the silent treatment. Your man can't read your mind; he won't know what's wrong unless you suck it up and tell him. A huge ego can and will lead you to a even bigger problem.

11. Not asking for what you want in bed. It can be as little as an appreciative moan when he does something good or as much as a frank discussion about your fantasies. Again, we can't read minds, and we'll both benefit from knowing what we find pleasurable!

12. Denying that there's a problem in your marriage or relationship, instead of facing it and asking yourselves what needs to be done. Problems don't usually go away on their own. Letting them fester only makes it worse.

13. Thinking that depending on someone else is a weakness. Leaning on someone else sometimes is the sign of a healthy relationship. Only thing about it is YOU do not want to use someone as a crutch but use EACH other as a foundation.

14. Over-analyzing. There's analysis and then there's over-analysis.

Wondering why the fiance didn't call once during his bachelor weekend in Vegas? A legitimate case for analysis. Wondering why he only called twice and not three times during a guys' night out? Not so much

15. Trying to reinvent the relationship wheel. If some items on this list feel cliche, it's because they are! If we would only listen to a good dose of love advice now and again, we'd probably save ourselves some heartache.

Ladies we are not looking for perfection just for the person who we can be perfect together with. Truly my opinion because I know a lot of guys looking for perfection and looking for someone who they walk all over. I love a strong woman with a voice but who will also allow me to be a man to the best of my ability. It makes me sick to my stomach when a woman gets into a new relationship and lets the sex change her. She stops seeing and talking to her friends or she neglects her child/children all over a stiff penis. Some women allow good sex to also change their behavior and they tend to start doing things out of the ordinary like live their lives before the sex was there. You can not allow a man to control you just because he has a big dick and a smile. Do not lose who you are, do not allow yourself to get lost in the "khaos" or forget that you are a woman! A strong woman who waited for a strong man to come around. Good sex is an incentive to a great relationship and shouldn't be taken for granted. I have seen some women lose their minds over a consistent supply of organisms. But why? I have no answer for that but I do know no real man will allow this to happen. Its about maintaining a balance ladies and knowing your worth as a woman. I have stated time and time again I can never tell a woman how to be a woman but I will tell you what I do not like and some of the things I know guys do not like. Yes me getting on the men is coming up but we're still discussing you. How many women do you know who lose their minds over sex? How many women do you know spend more time having "me time" with their man than their children? This shit has to stop! No one can stop it but yourself and if you allow the good D.I.C.K to run your life do not expect things to get better until you put it to an end.

Earlier in the chapter we discussed a list of relationship mistakes that women should stop making. The list was solid albeit a bit heavy on the progesterone but I can only write about what I see or have been through with women. At any rate, in the name of making this space of my chapter fair and honest I've compiled a list of things us men should probably quit doing in the name of health, love and relationships. We aren't perfect and we should squash a few relationship mistakes ourselves.

1. **Watching TV, reading, surfing the internet checking up on likes or retweets and/or listening to music during an important conversation:** Trust me, being able to recite the highlights (and a detail or two) of what she just said can go a long way. It's going to be tough if you have to ask yourself if she said it, or if you read it on a social network. Simple is better and paying attention may seem small but can go a long way.

2. **Showing improper levels of jealousy:** Some jealousy is good, natural and a bit flattering. Driving four hours to punch someone in the neck over a picture like over social networks is cause for concern.

3. **Trying to look too cool in front of your friends:** Yes, yes, bros before hoes (am I using that phrase correctly?). But this is your woman not a hoe. If you're mean to her in front of your buddies, they will not respect her. Not a good look for someone you say you care about.

4. **Thinking birth control is not your responsibility!** You are a man. Yes it takes two to tango but you have to take responsibility

to cover up or risk having a child. What makes it worst is the men who don't take responsibility after birth!

5. **Not being the same guy she fell for:** Now you're together. How do you relate to her? Do you take her on emotional journeys and explore your connection sexually? Or is Friday night order-pizza-and-watch-TV skeet, skeet, skeet night? There's nothing wrong with getting comfortable in a relationship, but don't take her for granted either. She fell for the guy who was courting her. So take her on a date once in a while, like when you first met her. Make out with her. Remember how much you were dying to kiss her early on? How long you'd make out with her for? Spend 30-60 seconds per day making out with her. She's worth one free minute, isn't she? You wouldn't like it if she let go of her appearance once she became your girlfriend. She wants you to continue to be the same guy she fell for originally.

6. **Not making her look good:** Chris Rock stated "Women need food, water, and compliments. That's right! And an occasional pair of shoes" In general, women are more affected by others' opinions than men. And a woman's identity is (in general) more tied to her relationship status than a man's. So, go the extra mile to make her look good when her friends or family are involved. Swing those compliments not just in private but in public hell she's your woman. Even if she isn't in front of you make sure you let the world know how proud you are. No this isn't opening the door for the next fella to come have confidence dammit if she allows that to happen then she isn't the one for you. Give some unsolicited compliments about your girlfriend. It will make her feel so good (and her friends so jealous) to hear that even when she's not around, you are thinking of her. It will get back to her, I promise. Lastly dealing with your girlfriend's friends and family can be a big part of being a great boyfriend. Women constantly judge each other on their sexual

and romantic choices. One of the biggest gifts you can give your girl is to spare her the drama. She'll thank you for it – so it's a win-win-win!

7. **Being Too Nice:** When it comes to their relationship some men have a hard time saying no, eagerly trying to please their woman and not standing up to her. This is a double edged sword. If a man loves a woman, he more than anything wants to please her. Yet, if he turns into a push-over, it's the beginning of the end. Will women test a man's determination and will power? You bet! I was once a "yes man" and it got me nowhere! "Hey babe you this you need that etc etc over and over again or yeah we can do that" knowing damn well I was against it. The paradox is some women want you to stand your ground and put some force into the relationship, however, they will challenge you all the way there. If you can't show your strength, that woman will lose respect for you. The best cure for the 'nice game' is to have something to do that is so engaging and exciting that you simply don't have the time to always be around to be pushed around.

8. **Not Recognizing a Woman's Need for Balance and Harmony:** Men are masters of pain (just watch an action movie!), women are masters of pleasure. Women like to have fun, laugh, talk, cheer and giggle. They also love beauty & harmony blah, blah, JUST KIDDING! It's in their nature and it helps them recharge their batteries. Men we often shrug our shoulders when a woman insists on having the best room in a hotel, they take their time with picking the perfect seat in a restaurant, and expect the best service. Little do we know that it's in their livelihood: It makes them feel good and helps them to relax. Being too serious and thinking about problems is not their idea of having a good time. Not so for men. We love problems, the bigger, the better. A smart man let's his woman

have her way in choosing the right ambiance. He knows that when she is happy, he will be happy, too.

9. **Talking About Exes:** The female brain isn't wired like ours. They will actually shy away from you if you continue to tell them either how wonderful your ex was, how upset you are that she dumped you, how toxic your old relationship was, or how glad you are to "finally be rid of the bitch." Instead of being a turn-on, all this ex talk instantly screams that you have way too much baggage for their comfort levels. Not to mention the fact that it's boring for them to have a man whine on and on about a relationship that doesn't involve them. Get over it! And if you think you're still suffering from the dreaded "syndrome ex," swap dating, dinners and girls for the gym instead. And do this until you can, at least, go a whole week without mentioning the name of your ex.

10. **Not Listening:** Sound familiar? It's the No. 1 complaint women have about their partners. Men underestimate the power of simply listening, Love says. But it isn't all his fault. Women get a dopa-mine hit and build bonds through conversation. The average man doesn't get that same high. "Men don't understand that women talk to connect," Rochelle Levy (president of Aziza Publishing) says. "A man thinks she is talking to tell him something." And his natural tendency is to fix whatever problem the woman in his life is presenting... whether she asked for help or not. The Fix: Three simple words are magic for women, "Tell me more." And if you really want to sweeten the deal? "I'm interested."

11. **Not Offering Help:** Most women spend the day at the office, made dinner and fed the children. Is it too much to hope that we as men do the dishes without being asked? When a woman needs or wants help, she may not ask for it. No woman wants

to admit she can't live up to Superwoman expectations. A man who doesn't understand the power of the broom may feel the consequences in the bedroom. He doesn't understand that housework and sex are very related. How? For the average woman, housework pours cold water on foreplay. But seeing her man do housework? That's foreplay right now in some households. So what's a well-intentioned man to do? Look up from the TV and see what she is doing. Most likely, she's not relaxing. Is she doing chores? It's time to pitch in. Second, we need to remove the word "help" from our offers & just do it.

12. **Misunderstanding the 'Silent Treatment:** Fellas we think we're being punished when she gives us the cold shoulder. In reality, the silence means she's hurt and can't speak, or doesn't want to say the wrong thing. We also have it wrong when the silence lingers. We sometimes believe the wound has healed, but when she's not talking at all, the relationship has gone from bad to worse. Silence isn't a good sign, she may be making an exit plan. When a woman is quiet, a man needs to ask what's wrong. He needs to check on his partner and relationship. The magic words? "What's on your mind?" The best thing a man can do is reach out with compassion. It's key to making a woman feel safe enough to express her real emotions.

As a man I feel like women will never fully understand the true pressure we have on us. Granted tons of men come up with excuses on why they are not "stepping it up" whether its "my daddy wasn't around", "Bitch you are so complicated" or "I'm doing me so she better just do her". PAUSE! This is crazy and actually stupid and those three things are a few reasons women have no faith in us. But ladies some of you are very difficult to deal with; granted everything worth having is hard to get and keep but damn! As men we can not think just because we control the penis or D.I.C.K that we can just show up and not put in any work. We sometimes let our sex game or finances dictate how we treat women and this wrong! We can not think just because our penis is great that everything will fall into place. Life doesn't work this way As men we are the "providers", the head of the households, etc... but until we can accept that we have to work to make women believe this; these damn women WILL NEVER EVER understand. When we create excuses and continue proving them right WE look stupid as FUCK! We fail to realize that as "Kings & Queens" on this earth we have to work hard to cement the title.

How do we act like men? Easier said than done but here are a few ways I am learning to increase my manhood (no pun intended) and also how to further step my game up. The shit isn't easy especially with the women in 2013.

- **Make real decisions.** A man understands and respects the power of choice. He lives a life of his own creation. He knows that life stagnates when he fails to decide and flourishes when he chooses a clear path. When a man makes a decision, he opens the door he wants and closes the doors he doesn't want. He locks onto his target like a guided missile. A man doesn't require the approval of others. He's willing to follow his heart wherever it leads him. When a man is following his heart-centered path, it's of little consequence if the entire world is against him.

- **Be willing to fail.** A man is willing to make mistakes. He's willing to be wrong. He'd rather try and fail than do nothing at all! We have to learn how to grow more from failure than we do from success. Success cannot test the way that failure can. Success has its challenges, but a man learns more about himself when he takes on challenges that involve risk. When a man plays it safe, his vitality is lost, and he loses his edge.

- **Be confident.** A man speaks and acts with confidence. He owns his attitude. When the odds of success are clearly against him, he still exudes confidence. It isn't because he's ignorant or suffering from denial. It's because he's proving to himself that he has the strength to transcend his self-doubt. We have to be willing to be defeated by the world. Willing to be taken down by circumstances beyond our control. But refuse to be overwhelmed by his own self-doubt. He knows that when he stops trusting himself, he is surely lost.

- **Express love actively.** A man is an active giver of love, not a passive receiver. A man is the first to initiate a conversation, the first to ask for what's needed, and the first to say "I love you." We can no longer WAIT for women to take control! Its our job to share our love with the world. The woman in our life has to believe it! We have to make them believe

- **Face your fears.** For a man, being afraid of something is reason enough to do it. A man's fear is a call to be tested. When a man hides from his fears, he knows he's fallen out of alignment with his true self. He feels weak, depressed, and helpless. I have been through and recently trying to get over it. FUCK FEAR! I am so obsessed with proving fear wrong & I am not afraid to die for the truth about myself or success #FUCKFEAR Fear is for the weak and the weak are for people with no guidance you have to have the mentality EITHER I AM going to succeed or fail!

- **Accept responsibility for your relationships.** A man chooses his friends, lovers, and associates consciously. He actively seeks out the company of people who inspire and challenge him, and he willingly sheds those who hold him back. A man doesn't blame others for his relationship problems. We have to hold ourselves accountable for the relationships we allow into our lives behavior. We have to teach others how to treat us by the relationships we are willing to allow into our life. Seefucyalata to a life with negative or destructive relationships!

- **Die well.** A man's great challenge is to develop the inner strength to express his true self. He must learn to share his love with the world without holding back. When a man is satisfied that he's done that, he can make peace with death. But if he fails to do so, death becomes his enemy and haunts him all the days of his life. On a personal level I do not want to die in vain without leaving a awesome mark on this world!

Time waits for no man or woman! If you are interested in someone LET THEM KNOW! If you love someone LET THEM KNOW! If you no longer want to be with someone hmmmm LET THEM KNOW! Procrastination is the worst thing you can do to yourself or others; I said it in the first chapter communication, chemistry and consistency should be a great platform to use for your relationships. COMMUNICATION BEING VERY KEY. We are not mind readers and we can not predict the future of what others are going to do. Its scary because everyone wants to be happy but few want to put their hearts & energy at risk. I can't blame you; its not a good feeling knowing you are moving forward and the other person is at a standstill or moving backwards. We're human and we make mistakes but the biggest mistake we make is wasting our time on things we can control and wasting our energy on things that don't matter. We are guilty as a generation of not looking at the bigger picture with ourselves and our future. In conclusion:

Men: We have to step up! As a whole; women need security and they need to know that we are not a risk in the future. Granted some of these bone headed women don't know what they want and pretend to want the "perfect man" (NO SUCH THING LADIES) but we still have to be consistent and do our job. Our job is the shit we are not suppose to get credit for via awards. Listening to her, talking to her, not repeating our mistakes, not creating excuses, staying consistent with what made her fall for us in the first place & improving ourselves as men! Its quite simple and hard, because no woman knows the real pressure we have especially African American men in the USA. But we can not let that stop us from taking care of business. I don't know one man who doesn't want to be treated like a king; but as king you must handle the kingdom with pride; that means working your ass off so she has no worries about the finances, your loyalty or integrity. No more talking just do it!

Ladies: I know most of you are holding it down and I know some of you refuse to stop your ratchet, stupid & biggety bitch ways but I still love you. You want a good man right? Then show him, appreciate that man with everything you have, he will NEVER BE PERFECT! NEVER! Get that shit out of your head NOW PLEASE don't worry I'll wait *waiting* OK moving on. You are beautiful THE BEST thing put on this earth as the mother of our children and the queens to our thrones. Its also your job to support us when we are down. Just as loudly as you complain and get on us for fucking up should be as loud as a compliment, words of encouragement and also praise. If you have a "ain't shit" man on your table then throw him away with the rest of the table scraps! Continue working on at your job & career REAL MEN can handle that. Don't throw in his face of the past or how you can do this by yourself. He's still a man who needs to know he doing his best unless he isn't of course. Its a two way street and you both are on equal ground. If he is giving his all follow suit & vice versa! No more talking just do it!

Overall we are fucking up as a generation. Not everyone will be married and not every relationship will last PROVE ME WRONG! As soon as you read this tell the person you are with how you truly feel even if it will make or break your commitment. We are all at war and something has to give. If you are going thru issues point them out to each other and fix them. Or leave them & each other alone. The choice is yours but I do tell you be careful; you may have a hidden gem & you might be with your next wife or husband.

Don't let sex control your relationships, don't lose yourself, and do not create excuses for stupid behavior. Get rid of "Khaos" do not let The good D.I.C.K control who you are. Deceptive Intuition Causing Khaos is nothing more than a wake up call that we are at war and the war must come to an end.

Dear Fear,

You are no longer welcomed in our community, households, or hearts! You have been a nuance for millions of years and its time we get rid of you. I know you may have your personal reasons for trying to creep in whenever you feel like it; but I write you this letter to know you are officially banned for life! Some may accept you but whoever gains hold of this letter have made a vow to no longer welcome you. I will make it my business to rid of you forever.

You were there after that tragic day 12 years ago in New York, you were there after my community reached an all time high rate of murders, you were there when a child could no longer trust the people around them, you were there when people turned their backs on faith!!!!!! You are a major problem and its time for you to go!

You are the cause of many relationships ending early, you are the reason people do not want to vote, you are the cause of non growth in my generation and you are why most of us stay stuck in the same position for years at a time. Its time we show you; you are no longer a factor in our lives! Its time we can look you in your eyes and say F*** YOU!

This letter is for that little girl who will grow up and continue of being afraid to move on, this is for the little boy who is facing the world by himself, this is for the elderly person afraid they may not get into heaven. This is for the people who donʌt know that their sin is no greater than the next person. This is for the people who donʌt want a commitment, who don't want to release their brand or music, who don't know that without you they WILL ACCOMPLISH EVERYTHING!

You are a non factor in a world full of future stars. You probably will not understand but then again that is no longer our problem.

Sincerely,

THE PEOPLE

F*** Fear

This is not a dress rehearsal this is it! LIVE YOUR LIFE! F*** Fear its not thinking about you so why think about it!? ON your time though but once you decide to do it DO NOT look back.

My generation is SCARED OF A LOT! From finances, marriage, commitment, success and failing.

During our next election lets get #Question99 on the ballot.

#Question99 is the fears that consume us all! We have to get rid of the fear! Fear is a state of mind that is accepted by the weak and expected from the doubters. THIS ISN'T YOU! You have to be willing to "die on a treadmill" in order to receive your happiness! If you are not pissed off for greatness that means you are ok with being mediocre NO DAYS OFF! Life is not promised for tomorrow, life is full of troubles, it's not gonna be so easy to fight but it's your life and you have to take the responsibility to fight for it. #F***Fear

#Question99 says we are all by ourselves! We can't do this alone I know this, I am a witness! There is a saying "the strength in the pack is the wolf & the strength in the wolf is the pack" Find a friend, love one, non judgmental person or especially if you fit under this category your faith! THATS what its there for, we must believe in something. It could be anything but you gotta believe this will soon come to pass. We have to remember that pain is temporary, go through it. Embrace and learn how to celebrate it because its going to take you to the next level: your career, relationships, your life etc...! Some of us are spoiled and haven't been through real shit a day in our lives yet and then get scared when it happens. Then they're some WHO know what pain feels like and KNOW that they can make it through anything. Stop being scared! Make a mistake but correct your mistakes its not about being perfect its about making the adjustments in YOUR LIFE! #F***Fear

#Question99 reminds you of your past. Your 'Past' is not your pass to fail. Do not allow what happened to you minutes ago, days ago, weeks ago, months ago or years ago be the reason for you not to strive toward success for your life. Stop looking for reasons to fail or find fault for your lacking and slacking. Your past is past, your present is present and your future like "All-State" is all in your hands! Don't waste time thinking about the little things that add up because they become a pile and a wall that you can't break down!! #F***Fear

Everything starts with US! *points at you* remember the "mirror talk" we had not too long ago? "Look yourself in the mirror every day before you leave for work and say these words to the person looking back at you. You don't need anyone to validate you. It doesn't matter who throws around their crap today or any other day - it can't touch you" #F***Fear

One thing that holds so many of us back is FEAR; It is fear of the unknown, FEAR of your feeling's, FEAR of rejection, FEAR of being loved. Don't let it stop you from living life; stop being so damn scared! Open up your heart, mind, and feel life because it can be beautiful if you let it!!!!! You are awesome! You are so damn powerful you have no idea. #F***Fear

VOTE NO TO QUESTION 99!

Another fear we have among my generation is having a legit family. I have learned that things have changed drastically. Growing up watching television, reading books and hearing stories from the generation before me that wanting to raise children, become married and build a legacy was the thing to do. Not so in 2013, I have been to more baby showers than weddings and have witnessed more divorces, breakups and broken families than sincere happiness. Why?? No seriously help me understand why.

In my opinion I believe not everyone will have children or be married. Nothing wrong with that, that is how the universe works at times. But I do have a problem with the people who block it from happening and those who destroy homes by being deadbeats, abusive, & just plain evil (yes evil). It is a choice and a honor to have a family, become married and building a great foundation. Some take it seriously while others could care less about it because they are focused just on themselves which at times can be very rewarding; but remember we were blessed to walk this earth to procreate and to extend evolution. Unfortunately they're some who just can't produce children or feel they don't have a lot to offer to bring in a spouse. How do we categorize those individuals? For those who can not produce children there's adoption, you can step up and help family and friends with their children, you can also volunteer in programs like "The Big Brothers & Sisters of America" program or at your local community center. The goal is help lead the future generation in a positive direction.

For those who feel like they have nothing to offer to a spouse just shut up or do something about it. That may be harsh to some and funny to others but the reality is nothing just comes to those who do nothing about it. You are special, unique and have tons to offer to people. What may work for others may not work for you (huge cliche) but its true.

Women: When will you as people and not individuals learn that just because all men stand up & pee doesn't mean they are all the same, when will you learn that just because you lay on your back and open up your legs and allow someone to ejaculate in your vagina that it will keep him around, for those few minutes yes but after that maybe maybe not. When will you learn that if you treat your vagina like a bad wall street broker it might plummet I can see it now "Pussy dropped again on the Dow Jones 34 points" stop giving it away too often and so easily. Make that man work! When will you know that its cooler to teach other young girls that fashion, clubbing, chasing men, chasing money & being a "gimme girl" IS NOT THE WAY TO GO! When will you realize that just because a man is being nice to you doesn't make him plastic (fake) pick your spots and be careful. A man seeks his wife and not the other way around. Give these men something to seek and not just what we see on television, in the movies or music videos. A real man knows what you are worth and will not go blind to a real woman. Stop being difficult all the time and actually listen to what men want; some women believe they know what men want and how they think. I laugh at this notion because you have not met every man. Yes its true most of us are simple but it is also true we can be a project waiting to be molded. Be patient, listen and make sure you are doing what is best for you while dating and going through prospects that will make a great husband.

Fellas: When will we AS PEOPLE NOT INDIVIDUALS learn that just because we have a penis that we don't control who stays in or out in our relationships! We need to learn that saying the words "I'm sorry" become null & void after we use them so many times its like saying good morning or good night the words become useless! No woman wants a sorry man! SORRY! When will we know the difference between hustlin' & grindin'? Hustlin' will come back to get you and bite you the one that stinks and not the one that winks. Grindin' is the result of hard work and going thru the struggle of becoming successful while hustlin' is going thru shorts cuts and not learning a damn thing. Grindin' is doing what it takes to learn from the past. I love that so many people in Boston have dreams but EVERYONE isn't going to become a successful rapper or producer or promoter or drug dealer. Stop using New Jack City & mixtapes as a mentor, not saying stop but lets be real some of you just are not that good in certain departments and need to take up a new genre. We have to step up! As a whole; women need security and they need to know that we are not a risk in the future. Granted some of these bone headed women don't know what they want and pretend to want the "perfect man" (NO SUCH THING LADIES) but we still have to be consistent and do our job. Our job are the things we are not suppose to get credit for via awards. Listening to her, talking to her, not repeating our mistakes, not creating excuses, staying consistent with what made her fall for us in the first place & improving ourselves as men! Its quite simple and hard, because no woman knows the real pressure we have especially African American men in the USA. But we can not let that stop us from taking care of business. I don't know one man who doesn't want to be treated like a king; but as king you must handle the kingdom with pride; that means working your ass off so she has no worries about the finances, your loyalty or integrity.

EVERYONE: With relationships its all about effort! Its the most important part in a relationship! A relationship without effort is like a car without gas! Useless and disappointing! The relationship won't grow if both parties don't put time into it! Relationships are a two-way commitment! Helping each other out, little by little bit by bit Don't just let your man/woman do all the work! They will eventually get tired because it's clear you don't care enough; then its time to say SEEF**YALATA! Don't make yourself regret & question why you didn't appreciated their effort! For the most part sometimes all you have to do is just show up! Being yourself along with consistency & maximum effort from the beginning to two years into the commitment will go a long way. Who doesn't appreciate a hard working man or woman? You have to remind yourself that this is what you wanted from the very start & remind yourself about what you are willing to do keep that smile on your face. Work hard and play at the same time; you should be having fun with the person who you decided to put in your life. Remember they do not make you happy they are adding to your happiness and if they decide to f*** up you will eventually be happy without them.

We fear the fact we may end up single parents or being heartbroken. We accept certain things in our society like its ok to be a single parent. Granted things happen and you have no choice but that does not mean it has to be done! We celebrate the fact that we are doing it by ourselves at times; which is not a bad thing but when we get it to the point where women are being celebrated on Fathers Day and men are walking around not doing anything about it I have a huge problem with this. Contrary to a new cultural campaign by Hallmark, Facebook, Twitter and others, Father's Day is not a holiday for single moms! Here is a GREAT Father's Day present: a Merriam Webster's Collegiate Dictionary. Inside is the definition for father:

1. A man who has begotten a child.

2. A male PARENT.

3. A father-in-law, stepfather, or adoptive father.

I would give the dictionary to deadbeat dads, but I'd also give it to those being duped into honoring single mom's on Father's Day.

I once seen a "Happy Father's Day, Mom" in the Mahogany section I looked through the general Father's Day card section, but couldn't find the "mom" category. Why just the Mahogany section? Nationally, 1 out of 3 American children live in homes where fathers are absent, according to the Center for Disease Control. The black rate is 2 out of 3. The message to the black community is that single motherhood is acceptable, so celebrate with a Mahogany card? I have not said this in a while but SEEF**YALATA with all that.

There are many legit and even painful reasons beyond control for why moms end up raising a kid(s) alone: Abusive relationships, rapes, where the woman has to press through the pregnancy with much strength or even unfortunately where fiancés and husbands who die suddenly. However, there are adult reasons that happen within our control. According to a article I read via google Since the 1960s, increased divorces and out-of-wedlock births have dramatically spiked the number of households headed by single moms. And just like my father who didnt stay involved with his children, many dads cut and run. It's also true that many moms force fathers to stay away, reducing them to monthly paychecks.

I also understand that some children, whose dads aren't around, are often led to make Father's Day gifts for their single moms to make them feel better. Children don't need pity though, they're very resilient and can handle reality if you present it to them in the right way at the right time. Having them show appreciation for their next closest positive male role model an uncle, coach, pastor, or neighbor is a better option that could help replenish the value of men in the black community among future generations.

I respect dedicated single moms, but understand the definition. A woman can never be a father and a man can never be a mother. Both parenting roles are equally unique and invaluable. Even among same-sex parents, you've got two moms or two dads. The idea of Father's Day was actually inspired by a single dad who had to raise his six children after his wife died. Mother's Day is in May. You also have the lesser-known Single Parents' Day on March 21. By marketing to single moms on Father's Day, the role of dads is devalued, especially in a community that badly needs fathers to step up. Society should be lifting men who are honoring their role and not reminding us that there are some ass clowns posing as men BREAK THE CYCLE! Hence the reason some women are afraid of having children. This does give the ones who have babies with men who they know won't stay around a valid excuse. We have to be smarter with whom we give this opportunity to share our beds, bodies and feelings. I hate the excuse "I do not know how this happen" Ummm I do and I didn't even have to be there or know you. You put yourselves at risk for pregnancy the moment you don't use protection.

Fears with success often confuse me. Some have the talent but lack the drive because they fear they will fail. Some have the thoughts and ideas that will bring great success but will not put their foot forward because its not the "cool thing" to do. Some listen to others who tell them that certain things are not realistic; well it was not realistic to put two boards on a moving machine to try to make it fly but it happen. It was not realistic to speak to someone else without them being in front of you but guess what it happened. I was not realistic at one point for the black slaves to be free or to even have a black president of the greatest country in the world. It was not realistic for a woman to vote or for people to be cured of pollio but hey I guess you trying to fulfill your dream of owning your own business or perfecting your brand is just way too much. We get lazy and we also find ways to create multiple "reasons" for why we can not succeed. We point the finger at everyone but ourselves and we refuse to take full responsibility of our past. Your success can be accomplished by conquering your fear of what is stopping you. We forget that we have to fail, fail, fail, fail, fail, fail and fail some more before we succeed. Not every road is the right road but how would you know if you do not drive down it. My first book "Women R Stupid & Men R The Reason" was a great local success story; broke homeless man who has a large following finally releases a highly anticipated book. SUCCESS??? Yes and no. Did the book make the New York Best Sellers list? NO. Did the book help me climb out of debt? NO. Did the book solve our generational gap of stupidity? In some places YES, but overall I feel as if I could have done more planning, more marketing, more thinking and not burning a few bridges like I did with management, other brands, people around me and even with my audience. I have been in three relationships since releasing my first book and I have been on a roller coaster with results, almost equivalent to being in a glass case full of emotions; how can I release another book on relationships? I would ask myself this every night while writing this one. I should be scared on releasing, talking about or even thinking about helping anyone out. But I used that fear as a motivation. I used the fear as an example that we are not alone with the joys and pains in life. I used the fear of failing over and over again as a bar that I am not perfect and that I am a living witness that FEAR is nothing but a state of mind.

Fear can and will consume you if you allow it too. Fear will tell you that you can not be happy and that you can not get over your past. Some of us hold unto to things for far too long & where does it get you? Letting go is not giving up it is growing up: with your progress as an adult, your success & just life in general. Our fears are what fuel the negativity in the atmosphere. I always ask why can't people forgive and forget? Is this not a way of adding unto our fears that we will make the same mistakes or that will not learn from the past? Its hard for adults to admit when they are wrong especially if we are so passionate with our feelings and within ourselves. 2012 was a huge roller-coaster filled with emotions, tears, smiles, happy moments, depressing moments, revelations and the unfortunate death of loved ones. Through it all life is still moving along like the river of blood flowing through our bodies. Granted everyone celebrates & heals differently. Some will blame others for their actions, use their past and emotions for reasoning behind each event. Myself for example I take time to be angry, I will cry, I will yell, I will distant myself from everyone for a short amount of time & I will try to cope my pain with working out, prayer or writing.

What's crazy about life is everyone has felt the same pain; just in different ways. Everyone has experienced what it feels like to lose someone close to them, what it feels like to be rejected, be heartbroken, what it feels like to be the cause of pain & even being lied to or being the one lying. We are different yet the same in so many ways. So how do we move on without holding on to that burden?

Gandhi once said "The weak can never forgive. Forgiveness is the attribute of the strong" you can not feel sorry for yourself or others when pain comes into your life. You can definitely feel angry! Let it out! Let it be known that whatever happened to you that you are not happy about it. But accept it and move on. One of the loneliest and hurtful things that can happen to a person is being a victim or lies & infidelity. Another is losing someone close to you. Hell another being on top of your game at one moment then hitting rock bottom the next. All of these have happen to me within the past two years. Yet here I am bouncing back stronger than ever again.

It takes a strong person to learn from their mistakes and become an even better person after. If we could only see our lives in reverse, we would not waste a minute dwelling and waiting for time that is always late on arrival. The easy thing to do is dwell on what happened to you & let that change you in a negative aspect. Don't go down that road! Its pointless and will stunt your growth as a man/ woman. The secret is you do not have to put up with the bullshit of your past! If someone made the decision to walk out of your life SEEF**YALATA! If someone decided to lie to you, cheat on you, abuse you, etc etc SEEF**YALATA! Its easier said than done but your life will be much easier and better without them. I hate to say this but some people do actually deserve some of the pain they go through. Why? 1. They are probably doing wrong in the first place 2. They decided to put up with the bullshit 3. They are too weak to say f*** you I can not to do this I am out!

I say this loud a clear F*** Fear! Fear will not be the demise of my generation if we take a stand and if we realize it is not too late for change, consistency and the willingness to recognize where we need to grow. The best way to live a happy life is to create one! Point blank there is no reason to have a plan B because it distracts from plan A I thank God for the alphabet because if I had stuck to just plan B, I wouldn't have made it this far. After you work hard at overcoming your fears just try to do the right thing and live by your principles on a daily basis; practice consistent progression not perfection when it is all said and done don't just leave a legacy, be a legacy.

Here a story told in almost every neighborhood nationwide

"On April 6th, 2009 my sister Charline Rosemond fails to come home. At first we think she's decided to stay out extremely late and will be home in any minute. But she doesn't show up to work and we know something is wrong! At this time I am 8 months pregnant and also not speaking to my sister (petty sister argument) My family and I begin to search for her. We go to the Police station and they tell us she is an adult so she may not technically be missing but we try and convince them that something is wrong. Our cries fall on deaf ears. We begin to do our own investigation to find my missing sister. I come to learn that she was with a friend that said he would help her buy a car. My sister also left the house that morning with $4,000 cash on her. I go to the friend's house and speak to him and he claims to have never seen her. 6 LONG days go by and not a word from my sister and no one has seen her.

My 21st birthday came and went (April 11th, 2009) and still we can't find her. Then on the evening of Apr 13th, 2009, we get a phone call telling us they've found my sister. She was dead, from one gun shot wound to the head in my father's car. The search finally came to an end. Unfortunately our search didn't end as we wanted it to. Till this day it breaks my heart that me and my sister, whom I lived with, weren't on speaking terms. But one thing I promise I will do is get my family and her the justice we deserve. Since her death, one arrest was made, and that was for perjury. He got 1 year and ½ in prison and has since been released. So in reality we haven't gotten anything! I pray that the people who killed my sister are caught.

I will end this by saying that this violence needs to stop. Especially this black on black crime. Too many young people are dying over nothing. Let's educate ourselves and work hard for what we want. Don't take from someone who's worked hard to get to where you wish you could be. May God bless each and every one of you.

Peace and Love,

Rosalie Rosemond"

www.charline-rosemond.memory-of.com/About.aspx

Franchise Player

*I*n another chapter "Man Up or STFU" I state "As men we must say to ourselves "I know who I am, I know what I believe in and I am willing to die for it". Some of us are content with being content and happy with the idea of being NORMAL!" As men we are a franchise we are the head of households, we are the standard and we have to set the bar for our families and relationships. I know some women are disagreeing; I could care less. This chapter is focused on the "Franchise Player" the man who comes through in the clutch, the guy who makes the sacrifice play for the team which is his family, relationship etc. I have been waiting forever to collect the knowledge and experience to be confident in writing this specific chapter.

Your 'Past' is not your pass to fail. Do not allow what happened to you minutes ago, days ago, weeks ago, months ago or years ago be the reason for you not to strive towards success for your life. Stop looking for reasons to fail or find fault for your lacking and slacking. Your past is past, your present is present and your future like "All-State" is all in your hands. Fellas I have said this time and time again its time we take control! Not do as I say control but I got this under control control. If that makes any type of sense. We love being in control and we love being the reason why something happen am I right or wrong? But until we has a whole step up no woman is going to be willing to follow us. How can we ourselves continue to be blind and expect to lead our families anywhere?

TIME TO MAN THE F*** UP!!!!!! End the "college/lets have fun/ I'm gonna do me etc' shit! WOMEN NEED MEN! Not us posing as men. Its not what they can do for us; its what we can do for them and then you'll notice change. NO MANIPULATION! Just transform from boy to man! Its not just about ourselves. What can you do to make her happy? Lead by example and if she doesn't follow suit then maybe she isn't the one for you! Its not what your mate can do for you; its what can you do for your mate. See what you need and be the person you want them to be but do not expect them not to be them.

Fellas I get it sometimes you feel overwhelmed to the point of breaking down. Sometimes you feel like giving up. And when you do, remember, it's okay to cry and to open up to others and when that's done, look in the mirror and smile. There's a reason you held on for so long with whatever struggles you went through whether if that was dealing with finances, relationships, your children or career. You can not give up! You are the FRANCHISE PLAYER! You are the one to take the clutch shot at the end of the game, you are the one who your family turns to when times get rough, you are the man who will take the responsibility even if you fail. We have to become better leaders starting with our homes.

Ok Steve what makes a great leader? Ask most people and they'll say "intelligence" for starters. Vision, drive, being able to communicate well, blah, blah, blah. Those are the crap answers you'll get from other authors who want to sugarcoat the truth and who orate from behind their oak desks. They're forgetting the big stuff; the stuff you don't learn sitting down while taking lessons.

What these "gurus" don't tell you is that the real traits that make a leader great are not the idealistic mantras or the status quo of "what a man should do". It's the stuff between the lines that only mistakes and experience can teach you. Sure, every leader needs brains (or in the case of certain chief executives, people around him with brains) and vision, but that's only to get the job. Staying at the top involves possessing completely different skills. Not every clown has them. What are they?

1. **Being respected.** You have earn your families respect and the only way you can do that is being honest at all times, you have to have the willingness to make mistakes and admit when you are wrong.

2. **Being street smart.** It's self-explanatory, if I need to explain it, you'll never have it.

3. **Being feared.** No not in the way where you are abusive or to the point where your wife or kids are afraid to speak to you but make sure they know who is boss by disciplining your kids effectively so their minor mistakes become extinct. With your wife well thats a battle we will never win so just accept it!

4. **Getting your fingernails dirty.** Leading by example. If you tell your kids don't leave dishes in the sink you don't either, if you tell your wife to stop leaving the room a mess you don't either! Etc etc lead by example and not by just words

5. **Leading spiritually.** How can and should you spiritually lead your wife and children? To accomplish this task you first must be a spiritually committed man. It is obvious that you cannot lead anyone anywhere if you have not been there first. This is what Jesus meant when he reproved the Pharisees saying: "They are blind leaders of the blind. And if the blind leads the blind, both will fall into a ditch" (Matt. 15:14).

One of the greatest problems facing many families today is the lack of leadership by the husband. Some husbands don't realize that God has ordained them for this role, while others simply don't understand how they should lead; still others simply refuse to lead. Most of the men that I counsel or speak to do not realize that many of the serious problems that are occurring in their homes directly result from their failure to lead. It is clear that the lack of the husband's leadership in his home will definitely create a chain reaction of marital, financial, and parenting problems.

Many times men did not see good male leadership modeled in their own homes as they grew up. But fellas this is no excuse because once we become adults ourselves it is our jobs to choose our own fates and understand where we are in this world. I have also learned many men are just lazy and would rather relinquish the leadership in the home to their wives but why? Why take the easy route? I understand with our wives wherever we are weak they should have strength but overall guys? Wake up man.

Other husbands simply give up when their wives challenge them for the leadership of the home as their wives remind them of all their poor decisions in the past. I have been a witness of this and have also seen this in many households. How do we overcome this obstacle? Goes back to what I said earlier in "setting a fix" for our homes. Take the responsibility for our past mistakes and also figure out ways to correct those past mistakes. What sucks is I have seen men who are manipulated by their wives through tears, denial of sex, or constant verbal harassment to relinquish leadership. These are just some of the reasons I have found over the years that hinder men from taking the responsibility God has ordained for them as husbands. It is essential to understand that none of these reasons are valid excuses that God would ever accept for a husband not being the leader of his home. But we as men have to break the cycle!

Love is of great importance & that's why its importance can never be overemphasized. Love is a bond that solidifies marriages & it equally gives meaning to relationships in my opinion there is more to love than anyone can imagine you've got to love to live because life itself is a product of love. So loving your family, your wife and yourself is also a goal we should try to reach by any means necessary.

The goal is to be the best man we can be, the best provider, the best security, the best leader for our families. Stop letting these women take over our homes; but "your a man" SEEFUCYALATA! She's suppose to get on your nerves, shes suppose to nag & say "I got it", don't let her! Once you claim a commitment then commit yourself to man up or ship out. Yo franchise player 63% of youth who commit suicide, 90% runaway children, 75% of high school dropouts and 85% youth in prison all come from fatherless homes! Without our leadership your family becomes at risk for all of this. But fellas it is not enough to know how to be the leader in your home. You can know all the truth in the world and if you don't apply it in your life it is worthless.

You don't always have to struggle with life its not the end life is a relentless journey, not of mediocrity, but towards the impossible; you have to remind yourself that YOUR success and YOUR dreams are worth it! Tell yourself "If there are no limitations to my imaginations, then, there are no limitations to my success; I will die for this shit"! You are the franchise! You can accomplish anything you want man. Go after that job, live the life you want but stay responsible and honest. This chapter isn't to devalue the role for women in any way but to lift up that man whose manhood was questioned because he doesn't make enough money, who was cheated on, who was put down, who failed, who needs a pick me up, this is for the man who is tired of watching from the bench and wants to be that FRANCHISE PLAYER his family needs!

Fellas even if you do not have a family guess what within our communities you are still that franchise player. You are the man setting the example for other men. You are the bar that is set very high so your brothers, cousins, peers etc can say "Damn he did it so can I" .I don't care how corny that sounds that is a major accomplishment. You are the captain of your own ship and you are a leader within our streets, businesses, and churches. I can not stress the words "Franchise Player" enough. Don't let your words guide you! Your actions, grinding, & pursuing what the hell you want should guide you there are way too many of us are in neutral & not in drive.

It shouldn't take this chapter, my book or even my words via a speaking engagement to keep you on your toes franchise! Small things that you do in life stack up for bigger things; If you are lucky enough to find a way of life you love, you have to find the courage to live it, the goal is to make your name be worth more than your bank account. The goal is to also make sure that once you leave this earth you will be remembered in a positive way when there's no more life in you. Ask yourself "how will I be remembered?" Will it be for being mediocre and average or will it be for busting your tail for the things you want, for living your life to the fullest, for being happy and making others around you happy as well.

Our goal as men is to provide: security, stability, great sex game, & make sure she is happy! In return we get the big piece of chicken! Listen franchise this is your world! You can't not look. There is no other world. This is your world; it is your feast. You inherited this; you inherited these eyeballs; you inherited this world of color. Look at the greatness of the whole thing. Look! Don't hesitate. Open your eyes. Don't blink at what we have in front of us. Erase the following words from your vocabulary: contentment, struggle, fear and broke. It's said quite often from tons of speakers, writers and more if you can look up; you can get up!

No matter how hard life treats you as it should, no matter how dark the road ahead would seem as it would, always keep your head up! Even when it's hard to move, take small steps forward; especially in trying times, it's important to continuously push yourself forward because momentum is everything. Giving up is not the answer franchise it is not the solution to happiness, success or anything you truly want in life. We are very important pieces to this world and we have to overcome this huge cloud that is over the male community. Maybe I am not talking to you or maybe I am but I will say this; If you want to BE ALIVE in today's struggling era, you must BELIEVE in yourself did you know that courage is not the failure to recognize fear; it is the refusal to accept its offer THINK ABOUT IT & THEN CHANGE FOR THE BETTER. Men, let me say this as clearly as I can: you will be blessed and your family will be blessed if you become the leader that God has called you to be that FRANCHISE PLAYER!

To Kill or Not to Kill
Inspired by: Abortion

By: Mocha Dee

To Kill or not to kill...that is the question

I'm too young to be having sex

Not alone raise a child

I mean, some of my friends have done it

Some, more than once

The father don't want it, but he said it's my choice

I'm still in school, trying to graduate

But who am I to end its fate

Masshealth is willing to pay for it

My parents would call it a burden

But out in these streets they call it MURDER!

To kill or not to kill...is the question in mind

Just to think some one raped me

And left his seed behind

STDs checked out, but his semen clocked in

So now I have to make a decision that may kill my boyfriend

I mean, it's not the baby's fault that this situation happened in my life

But this situation will constantly haunt me when I look into its eyes

My family may understand that I need to get my life in order

But out in these streets they call it MURDER!

To kill or not to kill...I ask that all the time

Every time I go back I get chills down my spine

Hey, my man likes to go raw dog

He think of it as birth control

Once I said I wanted to keep it

He threatened to hit the road

So I want to keep him happy

Even if it sacrafices my pleasure

But out in these streets they call it MURDER!

To kill or not to kill...what the hell was I thinking

A one night stand and no B plan

I should've never done so much drinking

I don't even know this man like that

Not even sure if he'll believe the facts

That he's the father of my unborn child

What's the odds in that

I'm not in the right place to be a mother

I'm still having fun and loving another

Maybe I'll have one when life's a little further

But out in these streets they call it MURDER!

You'll never know what situation you'll have in life

So always use a condom, always put up a fight

Because you could be next to have a dilemma of self will

And have to ask yourself

To kill or Not to Kill

Work Hard & Love Harder

When it comes to relationships the shit is hard work! One co-worker told me "Steven you want to get married huh? That will be the hardest thing you ever go through in your life! Its not a bad thing if the both of you are on the same page and if the both of you learn how not to always want to be right". At first I'm like get the hell out of here why wouldn't I want to be right if I know I'm right? Then I contemplated and thought he is absolutely right; if I'm right yet we are still torn apart who in the blue hell wins? In this chapter we are going to explore the hardships of actually working hard in your commitment, what are you willing to sacrifice? What are you willing to take? What are you willing to give? What are you willing to go through? How can you maintain a healthy commitment without losing the person you are? If everything is "good" how can you become great?! and What does it take to get to the next level?

Its crazy because during my first book "Women R Stupid & Men R the Reason" the only goal I wanted to accomplish was putting out the issues we have with each other and what to do to try to fix them when it came to relationships. I was actually in a relationship while finishing up the first book and that didn't go as planned. Tons of non fixable issues and I can not lie I got fed up to the point where the last month and half to three months I was totally mentally out of it. Which is not fair to anyone whatsoever so instead of forcing it to work out some more (staying that long wasn't cool) or losing myself, I left! Of course there are tons theories of why I left but it was because of my unhappiness and the fact I didn't see myself marrying this woman, nothing more nothing less. While beginning this book I was in another relationship that didn't last for multiple reasons. Nothing to gain by pointing fingers or using hearsay on my behalf so I will not touch base on it. Show's you once again we are all in this together; no relationship is perfect and every relationship has a expiration date whether if its via death or breaking up.

When it comes to YOUR relationship, YOUR future, YOUR present, or YOUR legacy. Be careful who you share it with. When are some of you dummies going to realize that not everybody that you love will love you back? Be careful with who you love and who you share shit with; matter of fact make sure you know the meaning of love before you actually "fall in love"! The main issues we face with love and relationships are: most fall to quick, most don't know what the hell love is, most aren't ready & some are just down to play "house". In today's society love is a huge joke for example reality shows looking for love! Did I seriously miss the memo that said you'll find love by having ten to twelve men/women fight for your affection? You then narrow it down to who you are going to kiss & maybe have sex with until you figure who wins your heart? Damn I guess I've been doing it wrong with my courtship, learning and communicating with one fricking PERSON! We got the game so confused like dudes wearing dresses to proms. Stop letting Facebook & Twitter know what the hell is going on in your relationships also, this lets the wolves in and also can create arguments. Sometimes even the positive things can set you up for failure. Say if your happiness comes to an end then you may feel as if you have to explain yourself or you may have to lay low for a while until people get the picture that they have to mind their damn business. But once you place anything online its a open forum for any and everybody to say what the hell they want. YOU did it remember.

I'm pretty sure your friendships are very important to you and that your friends are looking out for your best interest but when it comes down to it the less they know about your commitment the better unless its coming to a final end. I say this because even if you are going through the motions and aren't broken up for good you do not want them (your friends and family) to picture your man/woman as the bad guy unless that's exactly what they are. But at times even the people closest to you can give you the worst advice ever and you may listen and ruin something great. Then again I have even told my friends "if they were that bad of person why didn't you say shit in the first place!?!?" So pick your spots with what you listen to and comprehend from your friends. Just avoid the tendency of listening to a friend(s) and then searching for things that are not there in the first place. You'll end up driving a huge wedge between the two of you and maybe he/she will also start to look at your friends differently. With friendships and your relationship make sure there friends get to know the real you and not a fantasy or terrible picture because of what they think they may know about you.

I don't know one successful relationship that didn't take hard work or that just cruised along until they had minimal issues. The shit is difficult and takes hard work hard got damn work. Some people can not handle the pressure nor can they overcome whatever issues may come there way, those people need to stay by themselves or find someone who they can walk over. Anything worth it will never be easy and any relationship that may seem perfect on the outside may have turmoil in the inside. You just never know especially when it comes to false advertisement via social networks and even club events which we will touch base on in the chapter "False Advertisement". As a generation we have the opportunity to really change the aspects of our commitments and the way we see them. Some women still think all men are the same and vice versa those people are f***ing idiots. Its like saying you had the chance to date every single man or woman out there which is impossible. Maybe its the people you find yourself interested in or maybe its you. Denial is at an all time high when it comes to those my age or younger sometimes even the older folks stay in denial about maybe they are not the person they think they are or pretend to be. We're in modern day genocide with our hearts, communities, homes and with ourselves. With every relationship whether if its in a commitment, with family or friendships if it ain't worth the fight then it ain't worth it at all. The moment you realize you are not perfect and that s*** happens to us all is the moment you realize life is too short to stress; better is a diamond with a flaw than a pebble without one. You are not perfect, you mess up and sometimes its you that has to change. We have to listen to our reflection at times and really see whats in the mirror. At times that could be "hey I have a real f***ed up attitude" or "dammit maybe I am being too picky" or even " yes! Lets stop driving people away with the thoughts of our past" You are your best friend and even your worst enemy; the choice is yours. Sometimes we have to punch life in the mouth before it gets a chance to swing on us and when you do hit it first hit life very very very hard. Some of us are so happy with being "good" that we don't think we can ever be great.

With relationships it's all about effort! It's the most important part in a relationship. A relationship without effort is like a car without gas just plain ole useless & disappointing The relationship won't grow if both parties don't put time into it. Relationships are a two-way commitment. Yes I am yelling again because I have too! I have made so many bad choices with commitments and during commitments that we have to HELP each other. Helping each other out, little by little bit by bit! Don't just let your man/woman do all the work. They will eventually get tired because it's clear you don't care enough; then it's time to say SEEFUCYALATA! Don't make yourself regret & question why you didn't appreciate their effort. For the most part sometimes all you have to do is just show up. Being you along with consistency & maximum effort from the beginning to two years into the commitment will go a long way. Who doesn't appreciate a hardworking man or woman? You have to remind yourself that this is what you wanted from the very start & remind yourself about what you are willing to do keep that smile on your face. Work hard and play at the same time; you should be having fun with the person who you decided to put in your life. Remember they do not make you happy they are adding to your happiness and if they decide to f*** up you will eventually be happy without them.

If you enjoy being single THERE IS NOTHING WRONG WITH THAT! Just continue being honest and do not bring anybody else down with your bullshit. Try not to block yourself; you have to remember once you get into a new relationship this person in your life is new so you have to teach them. No not take them by the hand and baby them but let them know what you expect from the relationship and what you don't like. That's where communication comes into play again; we discussed this in "Women R Stupid & Men R the Reason" communicating is more than just talking and wanting to be heard. When you assume that the person you are dating is just going to figure everything out on their own every time is very dangerous and will frustrate you but don't expect them to not tell you the same thing. It's all about give and take, you have to remember "hey this isn't just about me anymore" So I ask you what are you willing to do to get the relationship you want? Teach them how to love you and also learn to love them; I always say what is the point of getting into a relationship if you are not willing to fall in love? Why waste time just spending time together with no ending point? Marriage is the goal and its going to take hard work! DAMN!

Woosah! Definitely had a "moment" there because I am so passionate about this. We sometimes break up over the silliest things and sometimes we are very petty or shallow (read The Art of the Breakup) chapter to see what I mean. How many people do you talk to who want a successful marriage, a family and secure house and home? Do you think they get that with their good looks and actually keep it if that's the case? What makes a successful relationship last? I don't know! Maybe the three C's:

- **Chemistry**. Making sure you have a great understanding for each other, making sure you both are willing to sacrifice equally & the willingness to avoid bumping heads at all cost.

- **Communication**. Listening is the first way to communicate effectively. Pay attention to what the other has to say and also pay attention to how they express themselves and just pick up the little things about them by paying attention. Its also about expressing yourself without pointing the finger and getting your point across without anger or judgment. Granted we all have emotions that include rage, sadness and even shutting down when we feel our voice is being disregarded.

- **Consistency**. Really no punchline to this but CONSISTENCY to me may be the sexiest trait on a woman that isn't a body part. When you continue to build each other up and proceed to do the same things you did to attract them this can help your relationship. Consistency can be romancing him/her in different ways but still on the same path of their likes and dislikes. It can be only changing for the better and not being different in front of others. It could be feeling the same way about them whether if you or upset or not why should your love change unless of course infidelity is involved or you can no longer take the madness.

Many more factors but it's a start right? Communication may be the most crucial of them all. It's natural when you have a disagreement with someone or they or you do something that gets misinterpreted to explain and discuss what has happened. You can then move to a resolution and go forward if both of you empathize with one another's perspective and the incident/situation isn't showing any disrespect.

A relationship where you share similar values means it won't be like one of you is speaking Spanish and the other is speaking Creole but both assuming you're speaking the same language. In a relationship, you have the past as an indicator of the 'misunderstanding'. In a commitment, you have to question how much you need to really be explaining when you've been together for a hot minute. When you're re-explaining on a continuous basis, you're basically trying to raise someone from the ground up and also driving yourself insane in the process if you lack patience or have any doubts about being together.

Most adults know the fundamental difference between right and wrong, respect and disrespect, boundaries and no boundaries right? You wouldn't be shocked to those who could care less as long as their point is being made. Those who don't know the difference have serious issues that no amount of love or patience/emotional explanations and dogged loyalty can resolve. Explaining to someone how to treat you with the basics of love, care, trust and respect or repeatedly laying out why something doesn't work for you or is harmful, is incredibly devaluing. They show how much respect or lack of respect they want by nipping it in the bud or leaving you hanging. Or sticking to their "ground" and letting their ego not come up with any type of compromise or solution that can work for the both of you.

I hear annually "I'm not explaining myself to nobody" or "If I wanted kids I'd have them". You have different values and will see things differently from time to time but you have to realize you both are different. And if you are betting on potential and if you're not being treated how you say you want to be treated then don't expect things to go uphill. But if you see enough or feel too invested to back away then you'll probably going to disappoint yourself.

Just like the person who thinks that if they love enough that the other party will change and they'll reach a tipping point of reciprocation. When something isn't working for you to the point where you consider it to be a lack of care, trust, respect or love, you step and keep on stepping; trying to kill a dead horse will drive you crazy. If someone isn't going to treat you with respect further down the relationship or is giving the signs that they have no plans on changing then once again step! If you keep turning a blind eye, playing things down, or believing you can 'handle' it, you don't realize that you're actually inadvertently giving a thumbs up to and accepting what they do which let's them believe their feet are well and truly under the table when in reality your feet are a few steps out the door.

Some of us don't know what we are willing to sacrifice. We are so caught up on fairy tales, materials, finances and what we see on television that we lose ourselves in the bullshit before we can even take it to the next level in our commitments. Being comfortable and wanting financial security is very important but when we use that as a excuse to no longer love the one you claim you love where are we winning if we are not accomplishing it and leaving? If one of you has a issue with money then why can't the other step in and:

1. Assist them

2.Take control of that part of the relationship

3.Work with each other through a 3rd party.

Money will come and go, you can not take it with you once we die and if you allow it to control your relationship you will never be happy! Plan smart and implement a plan that will work out for the both of you in the long haul. I was in a few relationships where I was deemed as being "a broke n****" or did not care for my future because I thought about others around me, my house first or trying to get rid of my debt. I would love to continue investing in myself with the best clothes, shoes, and other material flashy things that I can't take into heaven when I go but I choose to focus on the bigger picture of things. I will make sure my rent and bills are paid before I stand in line for a fresh pair of the latest popular sneakers or video games. I am not the best financial planner and have been guilty of burning through money and living from check to check; mainly because of my past decisions coming back to haunt me. But does that stop me from loving or stop the person who says "I love you" from no longer loving me? Main point is if a person is busting their ass to do right and to get back on track with the goals you set out for the relationship why stop over money? Maybe its just me.

Love is hard! Very hard! And it will take a toll on a person/people. But you can not stop working hard that's the easy thing to do. You have to fight and you have to talk and fight some more at times. Loving each other is easy (if that makes any sense) let me explain. The art of love is hard but actually doing it should be easy. I have stated before that we nccd to get back to dating and having the men court the women. Remember when dating was innocent? The school dances? The love notes? Do you like me yes or no? Circle one. The crazy thing about it we're all grown up and all that shit no longer exist does it? Now its all about sex and more sex. I love having sex but once we let it dominate our minds we lose. Once we start giving it up so frequently and so easily we lose. Once we pretend that we don't need to work hard for it anymore we all lose!

I once asked via my twitter account if couples can have a healthy relationship without having sex. Does the love go out the window when sex dominates over love? Do we think we have to stop working hard once we zoom a zoom zoom in someone's boom boom? There are many opinions on this, but I'll say this because I think I've got enough years and experience in to give some insight on this one. I've been been having sex since May 16th 1999 which is no real big deal but hey its been fourteen years now do not judge me.

One long-term relationship I have had I was in I thought was the best I had ever been in. Sex was incredible, and we had everything in common. In the end however, when times got a bit rough for us, she bailed, and it tore me apart. After thinking long and hard, I realized that the sex was the only real base of our relationship to begin with, and I vowed that I'd never let that happen again. As a man that shit is hard!

Over the years I've realized that sex first relationships fail time and again, and that good, solid, long term relationships are not based on sex; in fact, it's those relationships that are heavily based on sex that usually don't wind up making it for very long. That's because while sex is an important part of a relationship, in the end it's how you navigate the bad times that really define how strong your relationship is. Too many people are willing to bail when bad times happen because it's easy to fix with a legal procedure and piece of paper, and sex is readily available elsewhere. In fact, over time if your relationship is based heavily on sex the boredom factor alone tends to lead people to cheat or split up, because they have no other solid foundation.

When I asked my mentor about how to stay married for a long time or even what the secret to a successful relationship is, I get response is this: Put off having sex with the person you've met for a month. If it lasts that long, then there's a good chance it'll succeed in the future, because you'll know that there are other things besides lust and hormones driving it. Guys lose interest after the conquest, so to speak, and many won't stick around without getting any va jay jay for a month. But at least you'll know why he left. Not saying your fucked up attitude, ugly bad ass kids or lack of patience didn't make this happen either.

Anyone who thinks sex is definitely important more than love, will probably end up being divorced or have their relationship come to a end soon. Sex is a very pleasureful experience and is a good thing to have in a relationship. But if your looking for something to last a lifetime, than basing sex as a very important factor in your relationship is not good. Very few keep the sexual pace up through their marriage. Everyone hits lulls and sex does drop off in frequency as the years go by. So sex is something that is to be enjoyed between each other but should not be something that is extremely important. Relationships that are based on sex as a high priority, rarely last.

Love and sex are not the same thing; this is something some people never learn. Sex without love is just physical. Love without sex can be pure, spiritual and true. But sex with someone you love unequivocally, can be gentle and tender, hot and wild, comfortable or simply sublime.

And don't ever forget that the most important sexual organ is the brain. I will try my best to mentally fuck the dog shit out of you if the case is we can't have sex. BUT!!!! I know from experience (myself) not having sex will frustrate people especially when you already started. Is is easier for women to turn down sex? Chris Rock said it best; "every woman in here, ever since you were young every guy you met has been trying to fuck you. That's right. Women are offered dick every day. Every woman in here … gets offered dick at least three times a week. Three times a day, shit! That's right, every time a man's being nice to you … all he's doing is offering dick. That's all it is. Can I get that for you? – How about some dick? Could I help you with that? – Could I help you to some dick? – Do you need some dick?"

In conclusion to that theory... DO NOT LET SEX DICTATE YOUR LOVE!

We are lazy as people and some will allow sex to control their lives with the "Power of the D.I.C.K (Deceptive Intuition Causing Khaos)" We are lazy, the first sight of trouble and some of us cringe up and quit on each other. We are also weak as a whole generation, we let television, music and social media run our relationships no no no not all of us but the majority of us. So I'll answer the question all over again "Steven what makes a good relationship work?" its simple HARD WORK. Our relationships are a huge cliché but very hard to keep trust me I know. What helps is to smile without condition; to talk without intention; to give without reason and to care without expectation is the beauty of any true relationship. Its EASY to start a relationship and harder to keep but just pray with each other, for each other and work hard to stay on the same page with each other. Learn how to bend! Once you and your spouse fight and you're trying to "win" but at the end of the day if the both of you aren't on one accord what the hell did you win? In a relationship its not about equal giving! Its about equal sacrifice! You each have a role to play that builds a great foundation. And even when you do get it right you are still going to have to return back to basics from time and time again. You'll bump heads and you'll fight but when you're working work and determined to stay on one accord nothing can break you. Remember you're not going to agree on everything just how men will never understand the things women go through is the same exact way women will never understand the things men go through we have to learn and just pay attention to each other; better is a built house together than an unstable foundation apart. Relationships in our generation fail because we look for each other to be a crutch than an actual foundation. So work hard and love harder.

Man Up or STFU

As men we must say to ourselves I know who I am, I know what I believe in and I am willing to die for it; some of us are content with being content and happy with the idea of being NORMAL!

Whether if you are single, in a commitment, married or just don't know what the fuck you want to do; as a adult its time to Man Up or Shut the Fuck Up (STFU)! No extra punch line to this method of thinking or way of living. I know for a fact you are tired of opportunities & situations passing you by or your significant other telling you to get it together. Are you going to continue bitching about the shoulda coulda wouldas or man the hell up and take care of business? When i say man up its deeper than "hey i'm a man now let me get up" let me make this loud and clear nobody cares! Nobody cares when you tweet every single issue you have, nobody cares when your current relationship isn't working out but you keep trying & trying to make something out of nothing, nobody cares when you are successful until they can get something out of you in return, nobody cares! The longer you talk the longer nobody cares! They could care less about the potential you may have, people could give two shits and a flying fruit cake about if you "want to do something or could have done this and that" without anything to show for it. Nobody fucking cares! Yes I said it! Just do it! Man up or STFU!

You have a circle of friends and family; keep them tighter than the pants our current teens wear and cherish them with everything you have but at the end of the day when the shit hits the fan who are they going to choose? You or themselves? Its nature and you can't get upset about that. That's not the point I am trying to make; what

I am saying is you are priority to yourself, you are very important and you need to step your game up and not worry about anyone's approval or a person not accepting you for who you are! Its time to take your game to the next level and want to succeed for you 1st, your family 2nd and then the future of your legacy. Everything else is null & void and maybe a possible bonus if they are an asset in your life. Other than that with most things its time to pull out your #seefucyalata button and press it again because nobody cares!

All the potential in the world doesn't make a difference without things to back it up. Once again nobody cares when you succeed without giving something away. Wait i take that back, they're plenty of people in your life who don't need or want anything in return; you need to keep those people around because they are dependable but before you get all joyful sit your happy ass down because they have a family and life of their own and please believe they will always come before you. Crazy thing that i learned in life is nobody really pays attention to 65% of the things you are right about but 100% of people will pay attention to you when you are wrong and will have no issue with telling you so.

You have a responsibility for being on this earth and fulfilling your every dream or at least try! Some of you wont even try and its a damn shame because you have so much to offer. Yes i just ranted. Nobody cares but you should! That was the whole point you need to care and fuck what everyone else thinks! We have to learn how to embrace life & make sure we live it to the fullest. We should treat life like a photograph; meaning we should live everyday as if we were living inside a picture, because after all, no one ever takes pictures of the bad times right?

As a man i feel like women will never fully understand the true pressure we have on us. Granted tons of men come up with excuses on why they are not "stepping it up" whether its "my daddy wasn't around", "bitch you are so complicated" or "I'm doing me so she better just do her" I have to use a popular acronym for Shaking my head multiple times on this one SMH! This is crazy and actually stupid and those three things are a few reasons women have no faith in us. But ladies some of you are very difficult to deal with; granted everything worth having is hard to get and keep. * **MESSAGE***

As men we are the "providers", the head of the households, etc etc etc but until we can accept that we have to work harder than ever to make women believe this; these damn women will never ever understand when we create excuses and continue proving them right we look stupid as all hell! We fail to realize that as "Kings & Queens" on this earth we have to work hard to cement the title. Chris Rock said it best:

"Relationships are hard, man. In order, for any relationship to work, both people have to be on the same page, both people have to have the same focus, and we all know what that page is. We all know what that focus is. In order for the relationship to work both people have to have the same focus, and what's that focus? That focus is all about HER! It's all about her! Fellas, when you wake up in the morning, you should look yourself in the mirror and say, "FUCK YOU!" Fuck your hopes, fuck your dreams, fuck your plans ... fuck everything you thought this life was going to bring to you. Now let's go out there and try to make this bitch happy"

GRANTED THESE ARE JOKES! But as men we must take a stand and remember that this is no longer just about us. We put up huge fronts via social networks and lose focus on reality. We act like babies when we don't get our way all the time or we create more excuses on why the relationship isn't working out. We blame everything but us! I have done this before and I am no longer afraid about the truth about myself as I have stated in the previous chapters.

How do we act like men? Easier said than done but here are a few ways I am learning to increase my manhood (no pun intended) and also how to further step my game up. The shit isn't easy especially with the women in 2014.

Make real decisions. As men we need to understand and respect the power of choice. We have to live a life of our own creation. We have to learn that life stagnates when we fail to decide and flourishes when we choose a certain path. When a man makes a decision, we open the doors we want and closes the doors we don't want. We must lock onto our target like a guided missile. A man doesn't require the approval of others. We have to be willing to follow our heart wherever it leads us and have no regrets whatsoever. When a man is following his heart-centered path, it's of little consequence if the entire world is against him.

Be willing to fail. We have to be willing to make mistakes. We have to accept that sometimes we will be wrong. You have to try and fail than do nothing at all! We have to learn how to grow more from failure than we do from success. Success cannot test the way that failure can. Success has its challenges, but a man learns more about himself when he takes on challenges that involve risk. When we play it safe, our vitality is lost, and we lose our edge.

Be Confident. A man speaks and acts with confidence. Own your attitude! When the odds of success are clearly against us, we must still exude confidence. It isn't because you are ignorant or suffering from denial. It's because you proving to yourself that you have the strength to transcend any self-doubt. We have to be willing to be defeated by the world. Willing to be taken down by circumstances beyond our control. But refuse to be overwhelmed by his own self-doubt. You must know that when you stop trusting yourself all may be lost. I had trouble doing this and had to learn the hard way confidence shows strength and sets an example.

Express love actively. As men we are givers of love, not a passive receiver. A man is the first to initiate a conversation, the first to ask for what's needed, and the first to say "I love you." We can no longer WAIT for women to take control! Its our job to share our love with the world. The woman in our life has to believe it! We have to make them believe it!

Face your fears. You have to remember from the previous chapters that FEAR is only a set of mind and that you are in control of your fears. Being afraid of something is reason enough to do it. When a man hides from his fears, he knows he's fallen out of alignment with his true self. I know you may feel weak, depressed, or helpless at times. I have been through and recently trying to get over it. FUCK FEAR! I am so obsessed with proving fear wrong & I am not afraid to die for the truth about myself or success (when reading this start a hash tag via twitter #FUCKFEAR) Fear is for the weak and the weak are for people with no guidance you have to have the mentality EITHER I AM going to succeed or fail!

Accept responsibility for your relationships. You must choose your friends, lovers, and associates consciously. We have to stop blaming others for our relationship problems. Or hiding behind excuses of our women. We have to hold ourselves accountable for the relationships we allow into our lives behavior. We have to teach others how to treat us by the relationships we are willing to allow into our life. Seefucyalata to a life with negative or destructive relationships!

Die well Our greatest challenge is to develop the inner strength to express our true selves. As adults we must learn to share our love with the world without holding back. When a man is satisfied that he's done that, he can make peace with death. But if he fails to do so, death becomes his enemy and haunts him all the days of his life. On a personal level I do not want to die in vain without leaving a awesome mark on this world! Hence the second book of this awesome trilogy.

These are not step by step things of being a "man" or even the only answers. Some will agree or some will disagree I don't care. As a man I have made drastic mistakes including after releasing my debut book "Women R Stupid & Men R the Reason" I have gone against my word on what I just stated in this chapter and learned from that mistake. But if my inconsistencies are continually consistent nobody will ever listen to me or even believe in me. As a man of God I had to learn the hard way and seek advice from the higher power. I am currently twenty-nine and will not be perfect but I will try to get better. I suggest any man or woman to do the same.

As we move with this chapter we also have to learn how to take our careers, jobs and activities as if we have nothing else to depend on. You never know if you can turn into that man/woman who is one pay check away from being homeless or jobless. Granted some of us are taking care of business and taking the proper precautions not to get into that type of situations but as I have stated previously shit happens and you are responsible to wipe your own ass.

I became homeless at one point because I became reckless and I became content with staying in one place of my life. I was all talk about releasing my first book with unrealistic dates and having events without having one chapter finished. Yes the book was also in production and I bust my ass with my notes and research, videos, blogs and concepts. But it meant nothing without a finished product! My job at the time paid very well and I just "knew" I was going to be OK, then a tornado meant a volcano and I was out of work without preparation or worrying. I had to man up. I had to take full responsibility for my actions and doing nothing until I had too.

I'll say it again God doesn't make any mistakes he doesn't put you through any storm unless he knew you could handle it. Sometimes he will put you through things just to see what you will do. Multiple

Grammy winner Adele was very successful with her debut album "19" and when her follow up album "21" came into production she received writers block and also lacked any type of creativity. Then her man broke up with her and proposed to someone else within a matter of weeks, she felt as if she hit rock bottom but something miraculously happened. Her pain turned into motivation and that motivation turned into a very successful album and six Grammy's! She went into the studio and produced the Best Album, Best Song, Best everything! This is what God does for us and it may seem like a huge contradiction that I am using profanity but it is true, she had to man up!

When I was sleeping on my best friends couch or seeking room at my grandmothers house my pain of not eating, not sleeping, not being able to think straight turned into motivation which turned into a very successful book. I thank everyone who read "Women R Stupid & Men R the Reason" Just know that every word in that book and in this one was very painful even while I was smiling.

As a generation we talk to damn much, we complain about things we are capable of changing & we have dug ourselves into a major hole. We are up next to take control. I was born in 1984 and I believe everyone born between 1980 & 1989 have a choice to either become phenomenal or become forgotten its that simple. We are having the children, becoming leaders in our communities, taking over as supervisors at our place of employment and some even opening their own businesses. But as a whole we are stuck in reverse. We are in a cycle where it is "OK" not to advance in life or where it cool to just do nothing. I remember offering a mens' type retreat on my Twitter account and the responses from a few guys at me shocked and disappointed and it wasn't the declining offers it was the reasoning behind them. Not all people are stuck but as a whole we really need to get our shit together.

With social media we share way to much & then wonder why we have no privacy. We share our meals, we share our inner secrets and sexual appetites, we share brushing our teeth or washing our asses. We have replaced telephone conversations and spending time with each other with tweets, reading Facebook status' and text messaging. No realistic way of asking someone how was their day in a sincere matter if we can read it online. We are quick to post pictures of our children before we even introduce them to their local relatives, every date we have with our significant other or accomplishment and I am guilty of this also. I only share the things I see or go through. No judgment whatsoever but we have to get it together. Ask yourself this "When was the last time I picked up a newspaper & read what was going on?" The fact at hand is we are so dependent on using the internet or our smart phones and lost base on doing actual research on anything! We believe EVERYTHING we hear via social networks and also have a way of starting silly rumors ourselves when we have little to no facts. Its a rotating cycle that must be stopped and that must end.

We aren't taking responsibility for our mistakes as a generation or as a community but what we do is point the finger at others or the generation before us and the generation after us. We talk about what should be done and what needs to happen but yet most of us just sit on our asses and do nothing. We tweet the issues quicker than we vote, we create Facebook status' more than we create solutions for the problems we face in our everyday lives.

When it comes to dating we have to honest, we have to be up front and we have to stick by our decisions. Honestly when it comes to break ups they are never final at the beginning unless you didn't love them in the first place, weren't really into the person or if its very early in the situation. Go to the chapter "The Art of the Break-Up" for more information. I said in my first book that marriage should be the goal for commitments and some agreed and disagreed which is no problem BUT when I see baby showers being more consistent than engagement parties it just gives me more motivation and material to work with.

Emmit Smith once said "All men are created equal, some just work harder in pre-season" I challenge you today and I also will ask those who have read this what did they come up with. I want you to go to the nearest mirror or anything with your reflection and repeat these words.

> **I am awesome!**
>
> **I will accept every challenge life throws my way!**
>
> **I make my own rules: 1+1 doesnt equal 2.**
> **It equals whatever I want it too!**
>
> **After today I will make sure I give my life every bit of energy I have!**

These words are simple but powerful, we have to understand that life is far too damn short to continue being content with the contentment of our boring lives. Yes some of us work a 9-5, take care of our children and more but what else can you do to achieve greatness? Some of us are happy with the current place in life we are in. NOT ME! Even with a book in over 250,000 stores worldwide and the sequel you are reading, I need and I want more! I always ask what are we willing to sacrifice to get it? Some of us care more about sleep, partying, our phones & entertainment more than we do success! Three of those things bring nothing more than a few hours of fun and a bill I'll share what I am willing to give up

Sleep. What's that? I don't do that anymore. I rest to keep my mind focused and my body healthy. Other than that I am so afraid I am going to miss the opportunity of something bigger than myself I stay up and work or think of ideas of things they need to be done my bedroom was once filled with posters of notes and ideas.

Phone. I only respond to the VIP in my life and business. I'm not rude to those who I am cool with but I cut people off when they try to discuss nonsense; I tell them to save it for someone else.

Entertainment. I only go out to network and when I need to rest my mind from working. I play ball with the fellas and hit the gym. I play video games and also do the family thing when it is needed.

Living is very infectious I am starting to love it again; its something you cant fake. I wake up every morning knowing I am willing to die for what I believe in! We have to stop running from our reflections & the problems we face ourselves. You are amazing! You are a warrior! You have come this far in life & there is no reason to turn back. Learn to STFU and handle your business with no excuses.

Men: We have to step up! As a whole; women need security and they need to know that we are not a risk in the future. Granted some of these bone headed women don't know what they want and pretend to want the "perfect man" (NO SUCH THING LADIES) but we still have to be consistent and do our job. Our job is the shit we are not suppose to get credit for via awards. Listening to her, talking to her, not repeating our mistakes, not creating excuses, staying consistent with what made her fall for us in the first place & improving ourselves as men! Its quite simple and hard, because no woman knows the real pressure we have especially African American men in the USA. But we can not let that stop us from taking care of business. I don't know one man who doesn't want to be treated like a king; but as king you must handle the kingdom with pride; that means working your ass off so she has no worries about the finances, your loyalty or integrity. No more talking just do it!

Ladies- I know most of you are holding it down and I know some of you refuse to stop your ratchet, stupid & biggety ways but I still love you. You want a good man right? Then show him, appreciate that man with everything you have, he will never be perfect! NEVER! Get that s*** out of your head now. Don't worry, I'll wait. *waiting* OK moving on. You are beautiful. THE BEST thing put on this earth as the mother of our children and the queens to our thrones. Its also your job to support us when we are down. Just as loudly as you complain and get on us for f***ing up should be as loud complimenting me us with words of encouragement and praise. If you have a "ain't shit" man on your table then throw him away with the rest of the table scraps! Continue working on at your job & career REAL MEN can handle that. Don't throw in his face of the past or how you can do this by yourself. He's still a man who needs to know he is doing his best unless he isn't of course. Its a two way street and you both are on equal ground. If he is giving his all then follow suit & vice versa! No more talking just do it!

Once again overall we are f***ing up as a generation. Not everyone will be married and not every relationship will last but I ask you to PROVE ME WRONG! As soon as you read this tell the person you are with how you truly feel even if it will make or break your commitment. We are all at war and something has to give. If you are going thru issues point them out to each other and fix them. Or leave them & each other alone. The choice is yours but I do tell you be careful; you may have a hidden gem & you might be with your next wife or husband. But just stop talking about what you are going to do or what you can do and just do it! Whether if its with relationships, your life, your kids, your career or anything its time for action and then documentation of what happen. Talk is cheaper than this book and cheaper than french fries sold at a corner store. I don't have any children or any on the way, the lady in my life does have one who I do give my energy & time to on a daily basis. I will never understand how a man or woman can bring a child into this world and not take care of them NO F***ING EXCUSES! But are quick to use social media to display them whenever they do get a chance by taking pics or using them as a scapegoat to draw attention. You do what it takes and whatever it takes to do your part. Not every relationship will work and you may make a terrible couple but that doesn't mean you should make terrible parents! Taking your child on weekends is also unacceptable you should be available 24/7 just as if the child lived with you. We accept this "oh he/she sees him/her on the weekend" bullshit! Yeah I said its bullshit! When are we going to grow the up? I blame the government in the 1960's when they created welfare/transitional assistance. Let me make this clear you ready? Transitional assistance is suppose to be transitional and temporary until you can get your shit together as a individual or family! Most take advantage of section-8, food stamps and child support! Yes you can raise your child by yourself BUT that doesn't mean its suppose to be done! Just because you can put a cat in the oven doesn't make it a biscuit be better and do better; I understand the father/mother of your child maybe the worse thing that has ever happen to you but as adults communication and compromise are the best steps; if all else fails PRAY! Stop posting about each other and just do something about it either fix the problems or move on. We talk to damn much. I have fallen victim to this and I pray that I have learned from my mistakes. Why do we only care about issues when s*** hits the fan? We only say "stop the violence" when someone is shot, stabbed, or killed? We comment on issues to try to fit in ESPECIALLY ON TWITTER AND FACEBOOK!!!! Word of advice if you are not knowledgeable on a subject STFU & get back to work! We also keep each other down when it doesn't benefit us financially or emotionally. No not you as an individual but US as a WHOLE! Once again we are the leaders we are about to hit our 30's or just passed our fun stage of college and being reckless. I don't think people are ready to really move forward in life. Life is to good for our society to be in turmoil some of us are way too blind to see it that way though. Its unfortunate we only come together to party or bury a friend or family member. Our motives are more towards fuckery like "Hoes in Boston" & coonery like making a fake account on Twitter or facebook about a killer, rapist or someone in the spotlight in a negative aspect. Overall MAN UP to our responsibilities, step up to the plate of the obstacles & problems we have with life or just SHUT THE F*** UP!

Sneakers in the Kitchen

During the summer of 1995 I had the pleasure of picking up a hobby by accident and something I will cherish for the rest of my life. I learned my way around the kitchen and I have been in love with it ever since I was forced to stay there during punishments from my grandmother Jetta and mother. The very first dish I learned wasn't fixing my own breakfast or lunch; that was too simple for me since I was only into cereal and bologna sandwiches. I learned to fix fried chicken and old fashion grits; not the instant 5 minute grits I am talking about the wait 20-25 minutes and keep stirring grits. Along with homemade biscuits and omelets, I had a huge appetite and after a while I had to fend for myself due towards the fact my mother was working late hours and I had to pick up a few more responsibilities around the house other than taking out the garbage and cleaning my room. In this chapter I am simply sharing a few of my favorite recipes. I will also share my progress from being lazy and settling with good and how I am still to this date on working on being great when it comes down to working out and taking care of my body. Some of the recipes are not for those who want to stay healthy unfortunately but they will definitely help with cravings, gatherings and Sunday dinners.

While growing up in Miami and living with my grandma Jetta Sunday dinners were always the best. Its a tradition I want to have with my family and have it passed down from generation to generation. Sitting down and having dinner with family should be cherished because we never know what can happen and it also takes away television, cell phones, social media and other nonsense that is getting in the way of our families being a strong unit. Having dinner together as a family allows you to talk and hold conversations, not saying you can't do this without stuffing your face but getting back to the basics of the old school will allow you to learn your children, spouse and even friends & other family members better. Most of the recipes I am sharing are basic! Some will already have their own twist on dishes like baked mac & cheese or pound cake. I get asked all the time to do a cookbook so this is the closest thing I can do please bare with me. I also dedicate this chapter/section to the woman who brought me into the kitchen my Mother, both of my grandmothers Hester Mae and Jetta Lee, a life coach/mentor of mines Shanel Cooper Sykes, & the many people who love when I trap myself in my kitchen. Granted even sharing the recipes does not guarantee you will learn how to cook but it should help with those who are single, who haven't stepped out of their own way when it comes down to cooking and for people who just want to learn the basics.

Lemon Pound Cake

- 2 cups all-purpose flour

- 1 teaspoon baking powder

- pinch of salt (optional)

- (2 sticks) butter, softened

- 1 cup sugar,

- 1 Shot of Rum (optional)

- 1 cup of confectioners sugar (glaze)

- 4 eggs

- 2 teaspoons pure vanilla extract

- 1/4 cup lemon juice or real lemon juice (I use real lemons), plus 1/3 cup (glaze)

Directions

1. Preheat the oven to 350 degrees F. Butter a bundt pan. In a

medium bowl, combine the flour, baking powder, and salt.

2. (using a hand mixer) cream the butter. Add 1 cup of the sugar and mix. With the mixer running at low speed, add the eggs one at a time. Add the vanilla. Add Rum

3. add the dry ingredients and 1/4 cup of the lemon juice to the butter mixture. Mix until just smooth.

4. Pour into the prepared pan and bake for maybe 45 minutes or until golden brown

Glaze

Combine the confectioners sugar and lemon juice until it is slightly thick and drizzle it over the cake

Baked Mac & Cheese

- 1 (8-oz.) package elbow macaroni

- 2 tablespoons butter

- 2 tablespoons all-purpose flour

- 1 cup of milk

- 1/2 cup of seasoning salt (optional)

- 1/2 teaspoon salt

- 1/2 teaspoon fresh ground black pepper

- 4 cups of Shredded Cheese (I use 4 different types mozzarella, white cheddar, Sharp cheddar & Swiss)

- Cheese Sauce (look below) Some use Velveeta but I am old fashion

Directions

1. Prepare pasta according to package directions. Keep warm.

2. Melt butter in a large saucepan or Dutch oven over medium-low heat; whisk in flour until smooth. Cook, whisking constantly, 2 minutes. Gradually whisk in milk, and cook, whisking constantly, 5 minutes or until thickened. Remove from heat. Stir in salt, black and seasoning salt, 2 cups of shredded cheese, and cooked pasta. Add Cheese Sauce (look below)

3. Spoon pasta mixture into a lightly greased 2-qt. baking dish; top with remaining 2 cups of cheese.

4. Bake at 400°F for 20 minutes or until bubbly. Let stand 10 minutes before serving

Cheese Sauce

Heat 1 teaspoon of oil in a saute pan over medium heat. Add the 3 tablespoons of butter and stir in with a whisk. When butter is melted, add the 3 tbsp of flour and whisk the flour in with the butter until the flour cooks fully and no longer looks white. The flour might clump up but that is ok. Add the liquid about 1 to 2 cups of milk and whisk to incorporate until all the lumps are gone and the sauce starts to thicken. Add salt and pepper to taste. Add ½ cup each of three of your favorite cheeses.

Cream Spinach

- 2 pounds fresh spinach, washed and tough stems removed

- 2 tablespoons unsalted butter

- 1/2 cup finely chopped shallots

- 1 teaspoon minced garlic

- 3/4 teaspoon salt

- 1/2 teaspoon freshly ground black pepper

- 1/4 teaspoon nutmeg

- 1/2 cup heavy cream

1. Bring a pot of salted water to a boil over high heat. Add the spinach and cook for 2 minutes. Drain in a fine mesh strainer, pressing with a large spoon to release as much water as possible. Finely chop and set aside.

2. Melt the butter in a medium saucepan over medium-high heat. Add the shallots and garlic and cook, stirring, until soft and fragrant, about 2 minutes. Add the spinach and cook, stirring, just until the liquid is released. Add the cream, salt, pepper, and nutmeg, and cook until the cream is reduced by half, about 4 minutes. Remove from the heat and serve immediately.

BBQ Buffalo Wings

- 5 lbs whole chicken wings, cut into pieces (one wing makes 2 pieces - the "flat" and the "drum")

- salt to taste

- 1 cup barbecue sauce (I use Sweet Baby Rays)

- 1/2 tbsp cider vinegar

- 1 cup of Red Hot hot sauce

- 1/2 tbsp fresh ground black pepper

- cayenne pepper to taste

Directions

Preheat oven to 450 degrees F

1. Cover two baking sheets with heavy-duty foil and spray lightly with non-stick oil. Season the wings with salt and spread out evenly on baking pans. Bake for about 20 minutes, remove and

turn the wings over; cook for another 15-20 minutes until the wings are cooked through and well-browned.

2. While the chicken wings are baking mix the rest of the ingredients in a large mixing bowl. Taste sauce and add more spice if so desired. After the wings are cooked, transfer into the bowl. Let sit for 3 minutes and toss again, repeat several times. The chicken wings will soak in the sauce as they rest, and the glaze will thicken slightly as it cools.

3. Toss well one last time and transfer to a serving platter. The wings should be well-coated with sauce, but not drippy. If you want, you can keep the wings in a warm oven (200 degrees F.) for 15 minutes for a "drier" chicken wing. Serve hot or warm at room tempature

BBQ Baked Beans

- 1 tablespoon olive oil

- 1 red bell pepper, chopped

- 1/2 onion, chopped

- 2 cloves garlic, chopped

- 2 (28-ounce) cans baked beans (Bush's Baked Beans any flavor)

- 1/2 cup brown sugar

- 1/4 cup molasses

- 1 cup Sweet Baby Rays BBQ sauce

- 1 cup paprika

- 1 cup sugar

- 3 tablespoons onion powder

Directions

Preheat oven to 275 degrees F

In a large Dutch oven or pot, heat oil over medium heat. Saute the red pepper, onion and garlic until softened, about 2 minutes. Add the baked beans and remaining ingredients and bring to a low simmer. Place beans in a aluminum pan and place in the preheated oven. Bake for 45 minutes.

Red Velvet Cake

- 2 1/2 cups all-purpose flour (recommended: White Lily)

- 1 teaspoon baking soda

- 1 teaspoon cocoa

- 1 1/2 cups granulated sugar

- 2 eggs

- 1 1/2 cups canola oil

- 1 teaspoon vinegar

- 1 (1-ounce) bottle red food coloring

- 1 teaspoon vanilla

- 1 cup buttermilk

Cream Cheese Frosting:

- 1/2 cup margarine

- 1 (8-ounce) package cream cheese

- 1 box confectioners' sugar, sifted

- 1/2 teaspoon vanilla

- 1 cup chopped lightly toasted pecans

Directions

Preheat oven to 350 degrees F. Grease and flour 3 (9-inch) round layer cake pans.

1. Sift flour, baking soda and cocoa powder together. Beat sugar and eggs together in a large bowl.

2. In a separate bowl mix together oil, vinegar, food coloring, and vanilla. Add to the bowl of eggs and sugar and beat until combined.

3. Add the flour mixture and the buttermilk to the wet mixture by alternating the buttermilk and dry ingredients. Always start with the flour and end with the flour.

4. Pour batter into pans. Bake for 25-30 minutes or until a cake tester inserted near the middle comes out clean but be careful not to over bake or you'll end up with a dry cake.

5. cool for about 10 minutes before turning out of pan. Cool completely before frosting.

Cream Cheese Frosting:

Let margarine and cream cheese soften to room temperature. Cream well. Add sugar and beat until mixed but not so much that the frosting becomes "loose". Add vanilla and nuts. Spread between layers and on top and sides of cake.

Cheesecake Brownies

Cheesecake topping:

*   8 ounces of Philadelphia cream cheese

- 1/3 cup sugar

- 1/2 teaspoon vanilla extract

- 1 large egg

Brownie Layer:

- 2 ounces semisweet chocolate, chopped

- 3 tablespoons unsalted butter

- 2 tablespoons canola oil

- 1 cup all-purpose flour

- 1/2 cup unsweetened Dutch-process cocoa powder

- 1 teaspoon baking powder

- 1/2 teaspoon fine sea salt

- 3/4 cup packed dark brown sugar

- 1/4 cup granulated sugar

- 1/2 cup lowfat buttermilk

- 2 large egg whites

- 2 teaspoons vanilla extract

Directions

Preheat the oven to 350 degrees F.

1. Line an 8 by 8-inch baking pan with foil so it hangs over the edges by about 1-inch. Spray with cooking spray or coat with oil or butter.

2. *Cheesecake topping:* In a medium bowl and using an electric mixer at medium speed, beat the cream cheese until smooth and creamy for about a 1 minute. Beat in the sugar and the vanilla

until very smooth for maybe 1 to 2 minutes. Beat in the egg until well blended. Set aside.

3. *Brownie layer:* Put the chocolate, butter, and oil in a small microwave-safe bowl and heat in the microwave for about 30 seconds. Stir and microwave again until melted and smooth, about 30 seconds longer. (Alternatively, put the chocolate, butter, and oil in a small heatproof bowl. Bring a small saucepan filled with 1 inch or so of water to a very slow simmer; set the bowl over, not touching, the water, and stir occasionally, until melted and smooth.)

4. Combine the flour, cocoa powder, baking powder, and salt in a medium bowl.

5. Combine the brown sugar and granulated sugar in a large bowl. Whisk in the buttermilk, egg whites, and vanilla. Add the chocolate mixture and whisk vigorously until fully incorporated and the batter is thick and glossy. Gradually add the flour mixture and stir just until it disappears.

6. Reserve 1/2 cup brownie batter and set aside. Scrape the remaining brownie batter into the prepared pan. Pour the cheesecake mixture evenly over top. Drop the reserved brownie batter in large dollops over the topping. Draw the handle of a spoon through the two batters to create a swirled effect.

7. Bake until the top is just set, 40 to 45 minutes. Let the pan cool completely. Lift brownies out of the pan by the foil and peel off the foil. Spray a knife with cooking spray and cut into 2-inch squares.

Miami Stuffed Peppers

*   2 cups of water

*   1 cup uncooked white rice

- 3 large green bell peppers, halved and seeded

- 1 1/2 pounds lean ground beef

- 1 onion, diced

- 1 tablespoon of garlic powder

- Pinch of Salt

- Pinch of Black Ground Pepper

- 1 (15 ounce) can tomato sauce

- 2 cups finely shredded mozzarella cheese

Directions

1. In a medium saucepan, bring water to a boil. Add rice and stir. Reduce heat, cover and simmer for 20 minutes.

2. Preheat oven to 350 degrees F

3. Place green bell peppers in a medium saucepan with enough water to cover. Bring to a boil and cook for 10 minutes. Remove peppers from the water and set aside in a baking dish

4. In a large saucepan over medium heat, brown the ground beef; drain. Return to heat and mix in onion, cooked rice, garlic powder, salt and pepper. Pour in tomato sauce and mix thoroughly. Let simmer for about 10 minutes. Remove from heat

5. Spoon the meat mixture onto each half of the green peppers. Bake in the preheated oven for 45 minutes or until mixture begins to turn golden brown.

6. Sprinkle mozzarella cheese over the top of each stuffed pepper. Return to the oven and bake until cheese is lightly browned, about 5 to 10 minutes.

305 KONcept Jag

- 1 lb white rice, long grain
- 1 stick butter
- 1 med onion chopped
- 2 cloves garlic minced
- 3 tbs tomato sauce
- 2 bay leaves
- 2 tsp salt
- pinch of black pepper
- 1 can of kidney beans
- 3/4 of linguica (Portugese sausage)
- 4 1/2 cups water or as needed to cook rice

Directions

1. Melt butter in pot and saute onion and then garlic.

2. Add tomato sauce, bay leaves, salt and pepper and water and bring to a boil.

3. Add rice and bring to a boil again.

4. Cover and simmer.

5. In a frying pan, heat some oil, add beans and cut up sausage and cook a few minutes.

6. When rice is almost done, add sausage mixture and cover and simmer another 5 minutes or rice is cooked and done

Close to Church Biscuits

- 2 cups flour
- 4 teaspoons baking powder
- 1/2 teaspoon salt
- 2 teaspoons sugar
- 1 teaspoon cream of tartar
- 1/2 cup vegetable shortening
- 2/3 cup whole milk
- 1/4 cup butter, melted
- 1/3 cup honey

Directions

Preheat oven to 450°F.

1. Mix flour, baking powder, salt, sugar, and cream of tartar in a medium bowl.

2. Work the shortening into the flour mixture by crumbling with your hands until the mixture feels like cornmeal.

3. Pour milk into flour mixture and mix well.

4. On a lightly floured surface, knead the dough about 12-15 times.

5. Make dough into balls (about 2 inches) and place on baking sheet.

6. Brush Dough balls with some of the melted butter.

7. Bake 10-12 minutes or until golden.

8. Meanwhile Bring the remainder of the butter, and all of the honey to a boil in a saucepan, then set the honey butter aside.

9. When biscuits are done remove from the oven and immediately brush each biscuit with honey butter evenly.

Ciroc Pterodactyl Wings

- Peanut oil, for frying

- Kosher salt

- 1 teaspoon smoked paprika

- 1/2 teaspoon garlic powder

- 3 pounds chicken wings

- 1/2 stick (2 ounces) butter

- 2 cloves garlic, chopped

- 2 cups of peach ciroc vodka

- 3 cups hot sauce (Red Hot)

- ½ cup of peach preserves

- 1 tablespoon soy sauce

Directions

Preheat deep fryer with peanut oil to 350 degrees F.

Marinate chicken in 1 cup of the Peach Ciroc and 2 cups of Hot Sauce for 5-10 hours; punch holes using a fork so the alcohol and hot sauce can fully marinate.

Use full wings and cook them spreaded hence looking like Pterodactyl wings

Mix the 2 teaspoons salt, smoked paprika, and garlic powder

together in a small bowl.

Add chicken wings and toss to coat.

Melt the butter in medium saucepan over medium heat with the garlic.

Stir in peach preserves, remaining hot sauce & Peach Ciroc, and soy sauce. Cook until syrupy and thick, about 5 minutes. Transfer to a large bowl.

Add the wings to the deep fryer and fry until cooked through and golden and crisp, 12 to 15 minutes. You will need to do this in 2 batches so you don't overcrowd your fryer.

Remove the wings from the fryer and drain on a paper towel-lined baking tray.

Add the fried wings to the large bowl of sauce and toss until well combined and wings are well coated. remove the wings to a platter and serve immediately.

My Cornbread

- 1 cup all-purpose flour

- 1 cup yellow cornmeal

- 1 cup white sugar

- 1 teaspoon salt

- 3 1/2 teaspoons baking powder

- 1 egg

- 1 cup milk

- 1/3 cup vegetable oil

- 1 tbsp of Cinnamon

Directions

Preheat oven to 400 degrees F Spray or lightly grease a round pan or whatever you choose

1. In a large bowl, combine flour, cornmeal, sugar, salt and baking powder. Stir in egg, cinnamon, milk and vegetable oil until well combined. Pour batter into prepared pan.

2. Bake in preheated oven for 20 to 25 minutes, or until a toothpick inserted into the center of the loaf comes out clean.

As I stated before most of the recipes are quite simple but that does not mean that everyone can do them. I grew up eating the yummy foods my mother & grandmother cooked and picked up fast around the kitchen. Cooking for me became a private joy an underground pleasure. I was afraid to share it with anyone other than my family and expose myself to their judgment or being put to work. Slowly but surely, I learned to cook things that I could share and sell occasionally. I learned the old ways of cooking from my family members in Miami, FL. I studied food and went to local markets wherever I traveled deconstructing tastes from my senses alone. I learned all on my own that simply prepared, fresh, & homemade foods taste best. The recipes I have shared are mostly for small gatherings and events. Who knows I may just shock everyone and do a homeboy cooking show or cookbook. I urge for people especially those with families to cook 4-5 times a week and leave the microwave and take out alone. Nothing wrong with eating out or going to fancy restaurants but there is nothing like a home cooked meal prepared by your hands to supply your family or friends. Contact me on twitter @stevenabarthell if you decide to use any of my recipes or want to start a recipe club of sharing ideas.

The Art of the Breakup

*I*t's not you it's me. Or is it?

Just about all of us have heard or even said this line as a way of ending a romantic relationship. The problem is that it often leaves the "dumpee" thinking the exact opposite. Is there really a way to make a clean and honest break from a relationship? Is it ever okay to lie when ending a romantic relationship? Can you instant message him or her that it's over or do you need to do it in person? Is it really possible to be friends with your ex after a breakup?

You have to remember that all relationships are not created equal. "The nature of how to handle a breakup has to do with how you experience a relationship," says New York City-based psychoanalyst and psychotherapist Janice Lieberman, PhD, who specializes in relationship issues. For starters she says that not every relationship deserves a dramatic breakup. There are no hard and fast rules about what constitutes a relationship. "There are people who think they have a relationship with two dates and people who don't think they are in a relationship after 20 dates," she says. "If you have gone on one or two or even three dates, not calling is breaking up, but after some kind of romantic and sexual encounters, it is a courtesy to call," Lieberman says. Sometimes it's easier not to call, and there are people who will just run away. The explosion of internet dating has messed up relationships especially when an actual breakup is necessary. In this new era of social media and networking, people have Internet relationships (Twitter/Facebook) for a long time and then elevate to phone calls. Sometimes it takes a long time for a face-to-face formal meeting to take place. This can be problematic because people get very involved with each other and when they finally meet, there are a plethora cues that indicate they're not suited for one another.

Some of us have a tendency of breaking up with people the wrong damn way. Below is a list of how to break up with someone the right and wrong way.

Different strokes for different folks. The nature of how to handle a breakup has to do with how you experience previous relationships.

Break-up Do's & Don'ts

Don't Break Up Over Email: Rumor has it movie star Eddie Murphy broke up with Mel B. via a text message, and if this is true that is definitely a no-no. Text messages, emails, instant messenger, etc… are not the best way for ending a romantic relationship. Social networking sites, including MySpace and Facebook, allow users to post comments on each other's pages, but they should never be used to end a romantic relationship. EVER!

Stick to the Relationship Facts: Face-to-face or phone contact is a must, It's important to give the person you are ending the relationship the chance to ask questions and feel the sentiment underneath the words. Be as direct and honest as you can. Try not to engage in tit-for-tat arguments. Stick to the facts: "It's not working, it's no one's fault, and we need to make a change." Point blank period. There should be no sugar coating things and no feeling sorry for the person. You can't apologize for your feelings. Killing a dead horse will allow the situation to worsen.

Never be under the influence A little liquid courage might make taking the plunge a touch easier, but a sloppy split becomes all the more sloppy if you've had one or two drinks or a few too many. Being high is also, quite obviously a terrible idea. It is near guaranteed that breaking up will not go well if you're giggling uncontrollably, paranoid, or very mellowed out (personally would piss me off) This goes for them as well; if you know she/he is not all there, it's one of the worst ways to break up with someone. You want to make sure that you are both of sound mind when you're breaking the bad news.

CAN YOU BE FRIENDS WITH YOUR EX?

Whether or not two people can remain friends after a breakup depends on the two people and their feelings about the end of the relationship. If in your heart you really want to get back together, the best thing to do if the other person is not into it is to get out of it! You need time to detox and get in touch with yourself again. Talking every day as "friends" is a no-no. That just keeps hope open and setting yourself up for failure, Don't keep calling to 'check in,' or to hear how his or her day was, or if the cat is adjusting to their diet etc, etc, etc... Bullshit, bullshit, bullshit. Cut the cord in all ways.

Another no-no? Breakup sex! Just don't do it! Huh? Yeah I said it!

Write down five things you appreciated about this relationship that you would like to have in the next one, and five things you would not like to create next time. Instead of stalking your ex or making up excuses to call or see him or her, keep yourself busy with new activities, old friends, and healthy distractions. Don't get right into a new relationship, medicating your sadness with a new person isn't fair to either of you or them because you know damn well you can not and will not get over your last commitment without taking REAL TIME.

Don't go out with the huge cliches. Let's just be clear here. Saying:

"It's not you, it's me" is ridiculous. You're breaking up with them! You don't want to be with him/her! There's something (or some things) about them that you just aren't into anymore. Also, saying: "Let's be friends" is plain disrespectful. If you're ditching the situation, you owe her/him the respect of taking a step back. Leave her/him alone. If you ended it, you have no say on the friendship potential. That's their choice, and you need to suck it up, stay away and ditch the cliche mode as it is definitely one of the worst ways to break up with a person unless its a mutual agreement. If you are the one who decided that "Its Over" then make it over!

Remotely or via Telephone. Yes, this is the 21st century, but breaking up is pretty much stuck in the past. Don't even think about ending it online or via text message as we discussed this already. Phone call breakups have never been easy, so be a adult: Do it in person!

While on a date. Telling them that it's over before, during or after a date is the emotional equivalent of an ambush. It's just not honest. They'll know immediately that your plans were disingenuous because that's in fact exactly what they were. If the goal of the "meeting" is to finish the relationship, tell them that you need to discuss the relationship. Don't tell her/him you're going out for dinner or watching a movie and it doesn't matter what movie, because a post-date breakup is bound to have an unhappy ending. Once again this dishonest and very disrespectful. Even if they deserve the breakup or disrespect YOU are the bigger person and still a ADULT!

After A Major Life Event If you have any inkling that it might not be right, you don't want to be making any major moves like purchasing a house or a family pet especially a dog together. Or even before or after having a baby together or waiting until someone unfortunately passes away. Everyone knows that break ups are not a walk in the park, but it's also difficult to dissolve the partnership if you've decided to move in, buy your first house, purchase a car, or make any other investment together right before breaking up. It's never too late to end a bad situation, but why make it especially hard on both you and them by waiting even a minute too long and making it one of the worst ways to break up with a person?

By assumption. Sure, you're clear on how you feel, but you'd better be sure they are too. Don't take it for granted that a brief mention of how things aren't going terribly well will be accepted as an end to a commitment. What you say can be taken a number of different ways. You need to make sure that you limit this possibility for interpretation, so spell it out. Don't count on anything less than a clear statement that the relationship is done. If you're not saying it, they are not going to hear it. Then you'll end up with a crazy and deranged man or woman in your life because you couldn't come out and say how you felt fully.

In Public via a scene or party. Though from the outset, it may seem like a good idea to break the news in a public place, it's like a no-man's land, and that's just the problem. With public break ups there's no telling what might happen. In this situation, the event is simply not contained. If she /he gets upset, then you're responsible for making them upset in public. Fellas if a woman is angry, you look bad as as all hell! Public humiliation is never desirable (for you or them), so close the door to this possibility and stick to locations that offer you and your soon-to-be ex a level of privacy.

By cheating. It's guaranteed that it'll be over if they find out you have cheated (which is yet another ultimate sign of disrespect) but you'll also be forever known as the bastard, bitch, slut, hoe, asshole they caught cheating. It doesn't matter how much you want to get out, or how much another woman/man catches your attention or if it was a mistake you're bound to look bad if there's any awkward overlap. Also, once you've done the deed, you're technically available immediately, you'll probably want to wait it out a bit (like the notice you provide when leaving a job, a couple weeks is probably enough) before bouncing back into the dating scene or having sex with someone. A few hours or day shows you were not into them, loved them or even cared about the consequences.

Through avoidance. Again, clarity is the best policy. Yes, if you just quit answering phone calls, texts, e-mails, and your door, they will eventually find your ass or they will get the message, however, they are also bound to get mighty upset, and you should know this is the worst way to break up with anybody unless you're an extreme lover for punishment because it will take time and energy to dodge and weave between repeated cracks at communicating with this person. Man up and take the high road and end it with dignity. They'll most certainly still be hurt, but you won't be that "guy/lady" who was known for an being insensitive ass who won't pick up the phone.

When a little boy pesters a little girl, it usually means that he has a thing for her. If, instead of getting straight to the point, you turn pestering into provocation to locate a convenient moment to dissolve the partnership, this is going to be mighty confusing, annoying and angering for the person you are dealing with and it's one of the worst ways to break up with anybody. Sure, you may disagree over with something like television shows, music and who is more ratchet on social networks but if you make anything on this list the relationship-defining issue(s), you can count on being confirmed as extremely picky or just plain ole crazy. To be honest they are no real rules of breaking up with someone but the list speaks for itself; truth like rain don't give a f*** who it falls on. You may say to yourself well "Steven how should we break up with someone if I'm unhappy?" Well its easier said than done but here is yet another list:

Best Ways to breakup

Be honest. Everyone has heard the same old cliched lines before… "It's not you, it's me" its transparent and overdone. Nothing is worse than not knowing what the real reason was, even if it may hurt. Besides, Mark Twain said, "If you tell the truth, you don't have to remember anything." It's just easier. And don't get caught in a lie you'll just end up looking stupid.

Do it before you stray or eventually cheat. Do you really want to be that person who had to resort to cheating in order to let your significant other know that it's over? I didn't think so. If you're even thinking about straying, go ahead and address the situation you're already in before trying to find the "next thing" (which, by the way, won't be starting off on the right foot either). Exploring your options may feel thrilling or dangerous now, but trust me, it will never outweigh the guilt you'll feel later.

Listen. Even if you don't want to, do it. Even if you don't want to hear what they're saying, try. Even if you don't care, listen to this person for this small, defined time slot of your life. If you're breaking their heart, they deserve to be heard for a few final minutes with you. Who knows, you may actually learn a few things about yourself and what you need to work on in your next relationship or while staying single.

Do it in the right place. Once again that means: IN PRIVATE. Your soon-to-be-ex is already going to be heartbroken; please keep this from becoming the most embarrassing moment of their lives. No bars, no restaurants, no movie theaters, no parties. We discussed this in the previous list so try to think neutral: ideally a spot with no emotional attachment and ideally a day/time/place where it's easy for them to hear what you have to say, react how they want to, and promptly and discreetly leave the situation.

Don't delay it. When it is over, it's over. You know it so it's only fair to let your partner know as soon as you're sure. No one likes to be strung along. Don't think you're doing anyone any favors by delaying the inevitable.

Keep the Peace. Don't start a fight in hopes of lessening the guilt you may feel about breaking someone's heart. Know they'll be upset, so just stick to the end goal, which is to end things cleanly, fairly and honestly. Try not to make the other person suffer any more than necessary. Once they give you a rebuttal do not attack due to becoming defensive. Most people have this way of blaming the other person for why they are no longer happy; quiet as its kept sometimes it is them and not you!

Be Direct. Dancing around what you're trying to say will only open up the opportunity for debate and worse, begging and pleading, which may lead you to second guess yourself. Be clear, thorough, and offer to answer any questions. Leave no room for guesswork, which can be painful for the both of you.

Leave the scene. Once you've had this difficult conversation, honestly and directly, in the right place and time, with no fights, you're almost there. The aftermath is just as crucial as the actual breakup. Walk away, leave them alone!!!! Be a adult even if you run into them by accident and by all means, you made this bed, so be prepared to lie in it. Don't tease them about getting back together if you really have no intentions of doing so. If you have mutual friends just respect their space and time and if you have no mutual friends then leave them alone as well.

Sealing with breaking up with someone is the time-honored "Golden Rule." Leave as you would like to be left. Being dumped is a terrible thing, and if it's never happened to you, consider yourself lucky. Its happened to me twice before and sometimes it can leave you a empty feeling in your soul. Every relationship has a expiration date whether if that's a break-up or until death you part. Try to think about how you would want to be treated if the situation were reversed you'll end up with minimal regret and the ability to look back on the breakup and feel that you handled it in the best way you could.

I never understood why people cheat to end relationships or to do it thinking they'll get away with it. Why do men and women cheat? Is it boredom, thrill of the unknown or something deeper? And are any excuses even legitimate? I get asked this question during my workshops, online, book signings and social events and I could only come up with a few reasons because I have no idea. I believe you have to ask someone who cheated why did they do it and I can also speak from a man's point of view.

Reason #1

He/She ain't what she used to be.......I have read that the typical man can't resist the temptation of riper fruit, especially if the woman in his life has let herself go. "If she got physically lazy or gained weight or just doesn't take care of herself, a guy will start looking at other women," says Steve Santagati, author of *The Manual: A True Bad Boy Explains How Men Think, Date and Mate – and What Women Can Do to Come Out on Top*

Women who keep their men on a short leash need to take a "good, hard look in the mirror," he adds......Men should do the same. He might be a complete slob and still demand perfection from her. "It's the typical double standard," Santagati says. For their part, guys should try to rediscover the spark at home. "Make her feel pretty, even if you're lying," he advises. "Tell her how beautiful she is and how much you appreciate it. It will make her feel sexy, and she'll want to make you happy."

Reason or an excuse?_____

Reason #2

Familiarity has bred indifference. They feel taken for granted. Their guys will discuss the kids, bills and house repairs but they haven't really talked in a while.

To women, that failure to communicate translates to less intimacy and emotional and relationship satisfaction. When you're unhappy or dissatisfied in your relationship, you're more likely to be tempted to look elsewhere. She may begin to perceive opportunities like her cute co-worker, the flirty man at the store she attends on the regular etc. When a woman feels like little more than a household drudge, attention from someone else is extremely seductive.

Reason or an excuse?_____

Reason #3

No one loves a ball buster....... Perhaps nothing will drive a married/committed man into the arms of another woman faster than a nagging wife/girlfriend. She's like a mosquito he doesn't want to have sex with and he wants to swat her away. And go running for hot sex with a more "understanding" woman.

Reason or an excuse?_____

Reason #4: You're leading parallel lives..... You used to travel the same path, but lately your interests have diverged. Your guy wants to play video games with his crew or watch football in his free time; you'd rather go to festivals or watch some popular reality TV show. When you start doing things separately, you're more likely to meet others who share your interests. Soon you may have more in common with that guy/woman in your photography class than your significant other.

Reason or an
excuse?_____

Reason #5: It's just sex..... For most guys, sex and love are different things. Some really believe, "I can still love my wife and want to have sex with other women". That rationale allows guys to cheat guilt-free. If there is guilt, it may not be about the sex but the consequences. Will she kiss and tell? Will the wife find out? Thinking of cheating on your wife/girl? Consider the worst-case scenario: Your wife finds out and is brokenhearted, "Ask yourself, is it worth it??????" Its never WORTH IT!

Reason or an
excuse?_____

Yes the ultimate goal is marriage but if you are not happy then do not get stuck in a long term relationship or marry someone you do not want to spend the rest of your life with. Keep working hard at your relationship if it is worth it. The problem I see with our generation is we give up way to easily and also have no faith in each other. I do not see what the problem is with wanting to be married. Some stop themselves from moving forward together because of finances, some just do not see themselves with the person because they remind them of a parent or family member, and some people even stop from being married because they do not like the idea with being with someone for the rest of their lives. No judgment but damn where does the line end? I'm sure you've already heard that half of all marriages end in divorce. That statistic has been around since I can remember; you'd think it would've changed one way or the other by now. A dangerous statistic floating around in cyberspace right now discusses if happy couples get married or if getting married makes them happy. I believe that a couple should be happy first-getting married because you think the union will eventually make you happy isn't right. That sounds as if it is in the same ballpark as having a baby to fix an unhappy marriage, probably not a good idea.

A poll on Health and Behavior by the University of Texas states that although more Americans are waiting longer to get married that the odds of a lasting, happy marriage are more likely to occur if the bride is between the ages of 23 and 27, and age 27 for men. This is not meant to deter anyone who is over 30! Statistics are just numbers and should be used for maybe interesting dinner conversation and not something to base your future plans on. The good news is the over 80% polled stated that they felt that marriage should be a life long union.

A well known fact is that in previous history, people married very young, simply because we didn't live that long. During the 1800's it was not uncommon for people to marry in their mid-teens; in the 1400's you got married as young as 12 (A boy was considered a man, a girl was a woman as soon as she had her first menstrual cycle), something that was extremely common but would be viewed as scandalous in America today. Currently, Muslim girls can marry at age 12. Over 50 countries allow marriage at 16, including the United States. Some states require parental permission while others do not. Now that you know some of the facts and statistics surrounding marriage, you will be able to voice your opinion more articulately because you are educated on the subject. There is a difference sometimes between opinions and facts sometimes a huge difference and an informed opinion always hold more water than an ignorant one. Not everyone will be married or even spend the rest of their life with the person of their dreams. Its the reality of life that things will not always go our way and that some of us will die alone surrounded by family, our kids and maybe friends. Like I stated before they are no real ways to break up with someone just do not be a dumb ass about it like the letter below.

Dear My future ex lover,

The point of this letter is to let you know I am moving

on, our fun ended approximately three months prior to you reading this. I am only telling you what you already know, I donAt want to point the finger or say this is all you fault because it isnAt. I take full responsibility for my actions and I will take the blame for this whole ordeal. I am willing to answer any and every question you may have for me without hesitation. My heart just isnAt in it anymore, I refuse to live a lie and pretend that I am still in love with you. I havenAt been this unhappy in years; I shouldnAt have to feel guilty about wanting to be successful or doing whatever it takes to get there but thatAs all I got from you was the pity, soppy, woe is me sad story that I am sick & tired of. I will not hesitate anymore ITS OVER!

It was over when you missed the biggest night of my career, it was over when you told me on a consistent basis I was not needed for the most part, it was over when I came in sixth place to everything, it was over when my friends didnAt collect a bond with you, it was over when I learned you could never communicate with me the way I wanted to be communicated, it was over when your friends stated I wasnAt good enough for you, it was over when you tried to compete with me with our careers not realizing I was doing it for us and just not myself once I uttered the words I-F-U-C-K-I-N-G-L-O-V-E-Y-O-U!

I was done when I knew I could no longer give you the passion we spoke about, I was done when I found myself not wanting to be around your negativity, I was done when I said Awe have a issue and if we donAt fix it seefucyalata would be in the futureA. Please blame me for being honest, say its my fault for not willing to try anymore, tell everyone I ainAt shit for being a man and coming at you the correct way, burn me at the stake for telling you this and being a dick head and writing this letter. I am moving on and never felt better about it. It took four days to wanting to be with you, thirty-six more days to realize hey I am falling in love, eighty one days to notice you were still not embracing what I had to offer, one hundred & twenty-six days to prepare myself to fight for something that was never there, three hundred seventy-eight days to beat myself in the head and say this isn#t what I signed up for and one day to say seefucyalata. Enjoy your life and future endeavors of ruining someone elses time.

~Your future ex lover

Pain Is Temporary

*P*ain. Physical suffering or discomfort caused by illness or injury. Acute mental or emotional distress or suffering.

Pain is not permanent, it will not last forever and it will one day not be a factor in your life. They're many good environments people have destroyed because they believe they can not get over their pain. Pain is something that is universal and that affects us all. I'll be straight forward most of us are spoiled, some of us have not been through real pain or even faced strong challenges. Some of us are so used to having our parents, mentors or spouses bailing us out of trouble that we don't know what to do when we have to face them ourselves. Go through it, face it, fight it and then conquer the pain.

I have been homeless, heartbroken, lost, broke and thought life was over within seconds of being in two near fatal car crashes. I know what it feels like to have a five course meal in the best restaurants and I know how it feels like to go hungry or have to settle with eating grits and garlic bread so I wouldn't pass out. I can blame my father for not being there, I can point the finger at my past relationships, I could be stuck on "alright" and I could blame the color of my skin along with the neighborhood I grew up in but then what? With your pain its starts off with you; yes you! Even when it was someone else who gave you that pain. We have to remember we are in control of our lives and what we go through. Some of us put ourselves into situations knowing damn well the outcome is only going to bring us pain yet we still do it. Pain is temporary! Pain is temporary! Pain is TEMPORARY!!!!! Embed this into your mind, your heart, your soul, and within your new lifestyle "MY PAIN IS TEMPORARY!"

Life will hit you with a ton of bricks and bullshit if you do not have the right shield to protect you. Super Bowl morning of February 2012 I received a call from my father that made me numb "Steven, ummmm Anthony died this morning he's gone I'm sorry" I felt my whole brain and soul crush within a instant minute. This was the man I grew up with, the one who taught me how to play basketball and talk to girls even though I was a year older. I love him and I miss him dearly, hard not choking up writing this segment. I kept myself away from everyone for a while. The last time we spoke wasn't horrible but it wasn't great either funny thing is I don't even know what we were disagreeing over. Its funny how we are tested on a regular basis. I had to get back to the basics of my life, back to who I really am, I had to learn the hard way that when God speaks just shut up and listen! I lost a few friends and associates in 2012 & 2013, no love lost after reflecting on my actions and decisions. I am a grown man and if I make a bed I can either lay in it, flip the mattress or get rid of it (let that marinate). I would do things a lot differently with some of the choices I have made. But one thing I could not do was allow the pain to get to me. The pain of losing family and friends, the pain of things not going my way, the pain of starting over yet again and the pain of being close to losing myself.

After sleeping on my friends couch woke me up and I don't take anything for granted. That is one of the reasons I rather pay my rent and bills on time before I groom myself with fancy clothes or the latest sneakers so I do not have to experience that ever again. We have to channel our inner demons and face them head on and stop running away from our problems before they become bigger issues in our lives. You may feel heartbreak or loneliness or even frustration and wonder if you are going to be OK. You feel anxiety about the pain and wonder if the pain will ever stop and if you are going to survive it just remember there is not one person on this earth who has not been through it or won't go through it. We have to acknowledge that the pain exists. Stand back from it and get yourself unstuck from it. Try to experience your pain as a wave, coming and going. You may find it helpful to concentrate on some part of the pain, like how your body is feeling, or some image about it. Don't try to push the pain away. This makes it bigger, and increases our suffering. Don't reject the pain. Don't judge your pain or beat yourself over it. It is not good or bad. It is just there. There are no bad emotions, just emotions. Anger, fear, sadness are all painful emotions, but they are not bad. Everyone has them, and they are just as valid as the happy emotions you are human and are allowed to feel this way but at the same time, do not hang onto your emotion. Don't rehearse it over and over to yourself reliving every single detail while driving yourself crazy please don't escalate it or make it bigger whatever pain that is going on will soon come to pass trust me. Sometimes when we feel pain, like anger or a grief, we hold onto it, or we intensify it, making it stronger or bigger, in our efforts to deal with it or to give it our full attention. Just let it be there is no point in beating a dead horse over and over again hoping to bring it alive. Once we recognize the pain, cope with the pain, face the pain, it is then time to get rid of the pain! You have to remember that you are not your emotion and that your emotion is part of you, but it is not all of you. You are more than your pain, you are more than your problems and some fights are beyond our control.

Some of our emotional pains are difficult to deal with I understand that completely but what are you willing to do to overcome the heartbreaks and drama within yourself? I have noticed people often have a very low tolerance for the pain of heartache especially if it has happened time and time again they want to make it go away as fast as possible. And this is understandable. When you have a headache, you want to take something like Advil or Motrin to ease the pain; and if your body hurts, you want to rest, grab a massage or sleep as much as possible. So why wouldn't you want to do the same with relationships, friendships or dealing with partnerships at work? How Steven? Three ways Express, Suppress & Transform your pain into a distant memory.

Do you ever wish sometimes you had the right words to use beside f***, b****, s*** or anything else not found in the english dictionary to express what you feel? I know you have had words used against you by people who meant a lot to you and I know all of us have learned that words can hurt. Words can also help to heal, and words can often convey what you feel and make you feel better. The power of the "word" has always fascinated me. I have cussed tons of people out in my experiences growing up and as an adult. Sometimes I have not ok MOST times I have not used the right words to express myself clearly especially while being upset, being hurt, being torn, sad or even happy. So how can one really use the right words to express his/her pain? I can give you another list of things but will it really help? First and foremost know that crying is not a weakness! Let those tears flow, wash the pain away (no not literally) but let it out, scream, shout out what is wrong to the universe just do not let it store into your memory bank with no real chance for deposit. Write it out via a blog, diary or video using tactics of entertainment.

What you will not do is use social media as your therapy sessions that is a huge calling for attention and is not a good look remember you are a champion as we discussed in the previous chapters and last book. When you're feeling better you can look back at the entry and think, "How did this pain make me stronger?" Find a venting buddy someone who you trust the most or go see a person who will not be so emotionally attached to you like a therapist or counselor. You definitely want to give yourself time to go through these pains as well so if that means cutting off your family and friends for a while then do so BUT make sure you are focused on making sure you get away from the pain and putting an end to this feeling.

Family and friends make life so much better but allowing yourself to get fixed without distractions allows you to take your pain out on anyone & time to stare at yourself in the mirror to improve your decision making, allows you to clear your head and to reflect on not repeating what just happened to you. If your pain is related to a family member or friend passing away, do not forget them, but keep memories of them [pictures, home videos, favorite songs, etc.]. But do not sulk forever. The goal for overcoming these pains is to move forward with your life. If you are emotionally stressed about a person's actions or expectations, try talking to them and tell them what you're going through. If you are thinking about suicide, know it is not the only option. There are many resources available that can help you think of other ways to cope with emotional pain. Killing yourself is a permanent solution to a temporary problem. Also my friends you have to be mindful of those around you while venting; you don't want to accidentally take your anger out on an innocent bystander who had nothing to do with this pain.

Keep yourself busy while going through this, find a hobby or create a goal that will bring you success and happiness to replace this pain. Using myself as another example I wrote both books while going through pain in my life whether if it was a bad breakup, losing a family member like I stated earlier in the chapter or just going through losing a job etc. Use the pain to push you to things you never thought you could do. Use working out to tune out the negatives in your life, create music, poetry, a book of your own, website of what you went through to help others. Just do not turn to alcohol, drugs, physically hurting yourself or others. What you are also not going to do is avoiding these pains in your life, we just talked about this; you have to go through it! You have to experience what it feels like to be hurt, sad & torn because it is going to push you to greatness. These are only test to see if we are ready for the bigger things in life. This is what needs to happen before we can enjoy the fruits of labor and the happiness we are seeking.

Transforming our pain into happiness is not an easy task and sometimes it will take more than just the things I listed. Each person is different and will handle their pain differently than the next person, it depends on how strong you are mentally and spiritually in my opinion. Just like sex what works for one person is not going to work for the next person and we have to find our way to deal with our situations because at the end of the day its us (as in yourself) who has to deal with your pain! You will get through this no matter what because I believe in you, your friends believe in you and so does your family. So if they do not believe in you then they do not belong in your life. The bad news is that 'pain' happens but the good news is it will not last forever!

Confession of a Mistress

Poor little Wifey,

Home all alone

Waiting for her man,

Probably sitting by the phone

she calls so much,

I even know her ring-tone

but you out being a dog and tonight...

I'm the bone!

My name doesn't matter

but you know me by face,

You friend requested me

to see if he wrote on my page!

I know your suspicion must be driving you insane

you might be on his mind but I'M GIVING HIM BRAIN!!!

I do all the things that u just wont do!

That's why I'm on his mind even when he's with you!

Next time your out shopping, you should buy yourself a clue!

cause those marks around his neck...they came from me boo

That's how daddy likes it but u wouldn't know!

you're to busy worried about all these other hoes

but I'm right in your face, sitting front row!

Fuckin' ya man...and keepin' it on the low!!

You might be his misses but me I'm his MISTRESS

Whenever your not around, he's comin thru to hit this

I fulfill every fantasy he puts on his wish-list

There's no limit to what i do...

my skills are relentless!!!

We have ALL the things of any other relationship

yea we argue sometimes

But we're the best of friends!

All his boys know about me

and so does his kin

But they smile ya face, and chill in ya crib!

I could be a co-worker, or your very best friend

A neighbor a ex or even a relative

I could be anybody

that part is irrelevant

Pay attention sweetheart..

its the CONFESSIONS OF A MISTRESS

I've met your kids,

I know where you work

you think you gotta good man?

He really is a jerk

He told me he would leave if it wasn't for the kids

you think he's working late?

well he's at my crib

he tells me he loves me..

and I love him too!

But not even for a second

would I trade places with you

Because your truth is a lie

if only you knew!!!

The question is who's the mistress...

is it me or is it you???

ShaRae "Ms.Rae" Dulin

Who Am I?

I look into the mirror and at times I do not know who I am

Sometimes I am the voice of the voiceless spreading the gospel

of positivity and ways to improve our lives

other times I am a raging bull in a house full of glass tearing down the walls that I built

I hide the tears of my fears trying to be the leader I was bred to be

I am scared, scared of becoming a father, a husband and the head of unknown society

of speakers, leaders and individuals taking it to the next level

I am afraid of the same failures I tell others not to be terrified of

So who am I?

Am I the elephant in the room who will sound off vocal pipe bombs?

Am I the lion that roars obscene gestures as a defense mechanism to the ppl who love me?

Am I the wolf in sheeps clothing hiding from the flock & only appearing when its convenient

Who Am I?!?!?!?

Somedays I know other days I am lost

How can I lead with a limited identity?

Who will follow a man with many talents and more mistakes?

Am I the person I was born to be?

Am the loose cannon I am painted as when I am angry?

Am the softy when I am around children?

Am I the romantic lover & gentlemen?

The pressures of being a man are often overlooked and downgraded because of the

things "we're suppose to do" and how "we're suppose to act"

the frequent reminders of not becoming another statistic of unfit parent, spouse and black man

the constant focus of the microscope of are they practicing what they preach and so forth

At times I shatter that same mirror I am looking into mentally and in each piece I see a different reflection of myself but they are all asking the same question Who Am I?

KaniPublishing,Inc

11120 200th Street, Saint Albans, NY 11412
Phone: 347.548.0671
Email: dip_kanipublishinginc@yahoo.com
Twitter: @DIP_kanipublish
Website: www.kanipublishing.com

Now Is The Time To Get Your Ebook or Paperback Copy Of *BLACK GIRLS' HEARTS IN A POEM*....